Scribe Publications
THE NEW GRADED WORD-BOOK
FOR AUSTRALIAN SCHOOLS

Neil James was born in Cooma and educated in Sydney, where he completed a doctorate in English while working as an editor and a book reviewer. In 2003, Neil established the Plain English Foundation with Dr Peta Spear to improve the quality of Australian public language. The foundation has since trained some 10,000 professionals. Neil chairs the International Plain Language Working Group and features regularly in the media throughout Australia. His books include *Modern Manglish* (with Harold Scruby) and *Writing at Work*, and he has published more than 70 articles, reviews, and essays on language and literature.

THE NEW
GRADED
WORD - BOOK
FOR
AUSTRALIAN SCHOOLS
Junior and Senior Classes

by

W. FOSTER, M.A.
AND
H. BRYANT, B.A.

SCRIBE
Melbourne

Scribe Publications Pty Ltd
18–20 Edward St, Brunswick, Victoria, Australia 3056
Email: info@scribepub.com.au

First published by Scribe 2012
Reprinted 2012

Printed and bound in Australia by Griffin Press

The paper this book is printed on is certified against the Forest
Stewardship Council® Standards. Griffin Press holds FSC chain
of custody certification SGS-COC-005088. FSC promotes
environmentally responsible, socially beneficial and economically
viable management of the world's forests.

National Library of Australia
Cataloguing-in-Publication data

Foster, W. (William Charles Samuel).

The New Graded Word-Book for Australian Schools / W. Foster, H. Bryant;
foreword by Neil James.

Facsim. ed.

9781921844768 (pbk.)

1. English language–Orthography and spelling. 2. English language–
Composition and exercises. 3. Spellers.

Other Authors/Contributors: Bryant, Harold Clifford. James, Neil, 1966-

421.52

www.scribepublications.com.au

Making the Grade

Foster and Bryant's little word-book

Not long ago, a retail pharmacy proudly displayed a sign that read:

WE DISPENSE
WITH ACCURACY

When the local paper poked fun at the sign's double meaning, the pharmacist amended his text to read:

WE DON'T DISPENSE
WITH ACCURACY

Meanwhile, recruitment managers sifting the resumés of job applicants were sharing the following gems:

Career goal: I'm intrested to here more about the position. I'm working today in a furniture factory as a drawer.

Duties: My duties included cleaning the restrooms and seating the customers.

Skills: I am a rabid typist. I am very detail-oreinted.

Strengths: Ability to meet deadlines while maintaining composer.

Hobbies: Enjoy cooking Chinese and Italians.

More recently, a new breed of entrepreneur has emerged on the online auction site eBay, picking up 'camras', 'antiks' and 'labtops' cheaply before re-selling them with the correct spelling at a profit.

All of these examples highlight the problems that W. Foster and H. Bryant originally tackled in their graded word-book. As they explained:

> This book aims principally at remedying four defects noted in students — paucity of vocabulary, inability to spell correctly, carelessness in pronunciation and inexactness in sentence construction.

Half a century later, these problems are still with us. Even well-educated people trip up when spelling words such as:

bureaucracy

buoyant

dependent

embarrass

proprietary

rhythm

twelfth

For those of you feeling superior after reading that list, how confidently you could explain the differences between these words:

effect/affect

eminent/imminent

fish/fishes

imperial/imperious

licence/license

luxuriant/luxurious

practical/practicable

And could you identify the errors in these sentences?

The committee have decided to accept the plan.

Neither the table or the chair were broken.

My colleague and myself will attend the meeting.

I like explaining grammar more than punctuation.

Please take time to look over the brochure that is enclosed with your family.

More importantly, could you explain *why* these are errors? If you can't, this graded word-book will come in very handy, and you will find that you aren't alone.

A few years ago, the Royal Mail surveyed 1,000 people about the writing they receive from businesses. The survey found that 'bad design, poor grammar and atrocious spelling could be costing UK businesses a staggering £41 billion a year in lost sales'. Seventy-four per cent of consumers said that they wouldn't trust a business that used poor spelling and grammar.

The Royal Mail also found that 56 per cent of employees only used the spell checker when reviewing their documents, and a quarter lacked the confidence to correct their managers' grammar even when they knew something was wrong.

How did we get into such a mess? Largely by tossing grammar out of our school system one generation after Foster and Bryant last revised their little book. As a result, we've produced two generations of graduates without the apparatus to scrutinise their sentences.

We turned our backs on grammar for two reasons. First, it was argued, old-school grammar was taught in a prescriptive way using overly simplistic rules. While that was no doubt true in many classrooms, Foster and Bryant took a more balanced approach even then. They acknowledged that the 'makers of language are not the grammarians but the recognized writers'. But this does not devalue the currency of grammar:

> No man can hope to mould into an unalterable shape the English language. Nevertheless, we feel that the study of the rules, and the correction of the faulty sentences, will enable the student to avoid many of the careless expressions which are heard so frequently.

We wouldn't send people out into the world to be practising chemists without teaching them the difference between an element and a compound. Yet, like the pharmacist who dispensed with accuracy, we have been sending graduates into the working world without a clear understanding of nouns and verbs, adjectives and adverbs, prepositions and conjunctions, and the problems they present.

Happily, education authorities in Australia are returning to this more balanced view by restoring grammar as part of its first national curriculum. So Foster and Bryant are back.

The second charge laid against grammar was that it was drop-dead boring, a way of disciplining hormone-driven teenagers rather than giving them something of use. But today the grammarless generations clearly lament what they missed. The 10,000 professionals that the Plain English Foundation has trained rate grammar as the most enjoyable part of their writing course. This suggests that the teaching methods may have been at fault more than the grammar texts themselves.

So will you enjoy this re-release of a 60-year-old graded word-book?

It helps that this facsimile edition brings a retro charm. And what look like long, laborious lists of words turn out to be interactive exercises. Foster and Bryant teach grammar by inviting their readers to convert words between classes, turn them into plurals, correct faulty sentences, and substitute long phrases with single words.

My advice is to approach the book as a compendium of crossword clues, word games, and pub quiz questions. Because the book is graded, don't worry if you skip through some early pages until you settle into the level where your own grammar and spelling left off. You will find out whether you are grammatically smarter than a fifth-grader used to be.

Once you've established your level, dip in and out of the text rather than working through it doggedly. Test your knowledge by yourself, or with friends and family. By the time you have finished, you will have internalised the rules and terms of grammar without them sending you to sleep. Your sentences will sharpen and your confidence will grow. Before long, you may even find yourself offering (not dispensing) grammar advice to others that makes the grade.

THE NEW
GRADED
WORD - BOOK
FOR
AUSTRALIAN SCHOOLS

Introduction

THIS book aims principally at remedying four defects noted in students — paucity of vocabulary, inability to spell correctly, carelessness in pronunciation and inexactness in sentence construction.

Some of the methods employed to overcome these defects deserve comment.

Since it is incontestable that the majority of our students possess a limited vocabulary, such lists as "Verbs and their Nouns," "Nouns and their Adjectives" and "Adjectives and their Opposites" have been included. If these are treated as directed, linguistic knowledge should be expanded, and at the same time spelling accuracy assured.

Word lists, graded for various stages of the secondary course, have been given. These are resultant from personal investigation of the words commonly misspelt, and from a consideration of errors which have been found persistent in Australian, English and American schools. Lists, such as those recommended by the Sydney Teachers' College, the Victorian Department of Education and the Commonwealth Investigation Committee, are useful additions.

Suggestions are made for the pronunciation of many words causing difficulty. Unanimity in this particular cannot be obtained, but we desire to defend our conclusions on the ground that they have been reached after a consideration of the generally accepted pronunciations in Australia, and of the recommendations of recognized phoneticians.

It will be noticed that "spelling rules" have been rejected. To every so-called rule there are exceptions; we can almost agree with the foreigner learning English who declared: "The exceptions should be the rule." The advice given by a professor in Cambridge University is sound:

"There is now only one rule — a rule which is often carelessly but foolishly concealed from learners — namely, to go entirely by the LOOK of a word, and to spell it as we have seen it spelt in books."

An attempt to summarize the principal rules of syntax has been made. Some years ago, a grammarian wrote that "the adverb 'once' ought not to be used as a conjunction, equivalent to 'if once' or 'when once.' The custom has been springing up very recently in journalism, but is not sanctioned by literature." Recognized writers since the time of this grammarian have used "once" as a conjunction. The Oxford English Dictionary accepts the word as such, while Fowler maintains that "its use as a conjunction is sound enough, but it is sometimes forgotten that it is not for all contexts." Fowler's statement is further proof of our language's elasticity. The makers of language are not the grammarians, but the recognized writers.

Divergence from the accepted usage of a particular period can be effected only by a thorough knowledge of pure grammar of that period. This is our defence for outlining the ordinary rules of English grammar, as they appear to us. We have no doubt that some of our conclusions will be challenged. This is as it should be. No man can hope to mould into an unalterable shape the English language. Nevertheless, we feel that the study of the rules, and the correction of the faulty sentences, will enable the student to avoid many of the careless expressions which are heard so frequently.

The inclusion of new sections such as Vocabulary Expansion Exercises, Proverbs, Antonyms, Phrases into Words, and Idiomatic Expressions will provide students with sufficient material for the present progressive syllabuses and public examination papers of the Australian States.

Acknowledgement is made to the New South Wales Department of Education and the Victorian Department of Education for further reprints of questions from their Leaving Certificate and Intermediate Certificate Language Papers.

So that Australian teachers and students may compare their standards with those of recognized examining bodies in Great Britain, we have included Sentences for Correction from the General Certificate Language Papers (Ordinary Level) and Civil Service Examination Papers. For permission to reprint these, we express our thanks to the Local Examinations Syndicate (University of Cambridge), the Oxford and Cambridge Schools Examination Board, and Her Majesty's Stationery Office.

W.F.

H.B.

CONTENTS

VOCABULARY GROUPS

PRONUNCIATION GROUPS

CONTENTS

CORRECTION OF FAULTY SENTENCES

SPELLING LIST FOR FIRST YEAR

abroad
absolutely
accept
achieve
acquaintance
acquit
address
advice
aerial
aeroplane
again
all right
alley
ally
allot
allotted
aloud
allowed
already
altar
alter
although
altogether
always
analysis
angrily
appearance
argument
arrangement
article
artillery
athletics
attention
autumn
awful
awkward
baggage

balcony
balloon
banquet
barque
barrenness
bazaar
beginning
believe
besiege
bicycle
biscuit
bluish
boundary
buccaneer
buffalo
buoy
burglar
buried
business
calendar
cancel
cancelled
cannibal
canoe
caravan
carriage
casualty
cauliflower
cemetery
centre
certainty
changing
character
chieftain
chimney
chocolate
choir

climbed
clumsy
collision
colonel
column
coming
committee
completed
condemn
conqueror
convenient
corridor
courteous
cruelty
crystal
cupboard
curiosity
cutlass
deceit
decision
defence
denial
deny
descendant
describe
description
desperate
develop
development
difference
dine
dining
disappear
disappoint
disaster
disastrous
disease

doubtful
drowsy
duchess
dungeon
earnest
easy
easier
echoing
efficient
eighth
either
emperor
empty
emptiness
enemy
enemies
entitle
entrance
especially
essential
excel
excellent
excitement
expense
extravagant
extreme
familiar
fascinating
favourite
February
feminine
finally
forehead
foreign
forty
friend
frontier
gaily
galloped
ghost

glimpse
gnaw
god
goddess
good-bye
grammar
guard
haughty
heavily
height
heroes
heroism
hideous
holiday
honour
honourable
hoping
hopping
hungry
hurry
hurriedly
hymn
imaginary
immediately
incident
independence
industrious
interfere
interrupt
January
jewel
jewellery
journey
judgement
kernel
knight
knuckle
label
laid
lair

later
latter
laziness
league
library
librarian
lieutenant
lightning
lightening
lose
loose
loss
lovely
loveliest
lustre
lying
machinery
magician
magnificent
management
marriage
marvellous
medicine
merchant
mercy
merciful
merry
merrily
messenger
minute
miracle
mischievous
muscle
mystery
necessary
neither
neuter
neutral
niece
occasion

occupy	potato	relieve
occupies	poultry	relief
occurred	practice	religious
occurs	practise	remembrance
offer	prefer	remnant
offered	preferred	repentant
officer	presence	reply
opinion	presents	replies
opponent	prevail	rescue
opportunity	precede	rescuing
orchard	procedure	resistance
ought	proceed	retaliate
pay	procession	revelry
paid	professor	ridiculous
patience	profit	ruffian
patient	promptly	salmon
pavilion	propel	sandwich
peasant	propeller	sauce
penniless	properly	says
perceive	pumpkin	said
permanent	pursue	scene
permission	qualify	scheme
persuade	qualified	schooner
persuasion	quarrel	science
phrase	quarrelled	scissors
piano	quarts	scull
pigeon	quartz	skull
pioneer	quiet	secretary
piteous	quite	seize
pitiful	racquet	sentence
plague	really	separate
plain	rebellion	sergeant
plan	receipt	sewing
planed	receive	sowing
planned	recipe	shepherd
pleasant	recommend	sheriff
plentiful	refer	shield
poison	referred	shine
porridge	referee	shining
possess	regret	shoal

shoulder
shrapnel
shred
shriek
sickle
siege
similar
singeing
singing
skill
skilful
slyness
smoky
smuggle
solder
sole
soul
solemn
splendour
spoonful
stayed
stile
style
stony
storey
story
straight
strait
strenuous
subtract
succeed
successive
sufficient
supplies
surprise
surrender
swollen

syrup
taught
taut
telegraph
telephone
tenant
tepid
terrace
territory
testament
testify
thatched
theatre
their
there
theory
though
tidy
tidily
tied
tired
tobacco
torpedoes
transparent
travel
traveller
travelling
triumph
trough
truly
tunnel
tunnelling
twelfth
twentieth
tying
umbrella
unique

until
usually
vain
valiant
valleys
valuable
veil
vein
vengeance
view
villain
villein
violin
volcano
waist
waking
wallaby
warrior
waste
wearily
weather
whether
weight
wharf
wharves
which
witch
wooden
woolly
wreath
wreathe
wrench
wrestle
yacht
yield
yoke
yolk

SPELLING LIST FOR SECOND AND THIRD YEARS

aborigines
abyss
accidentally
acclaim
acclamation
accompany
accompanied
achievement
acquire
admittance
advantage
advantageous
adversary
advertisement
affair
agreeable
agreement
alight
allegiance
alliance
allowance
alms
altitude
ammunition
ancient
anecdote
annual
annually
anguish
anxiety
apparent
appetite
aquatic
archbishop
artesian
artificial
association
asphalt
asylum

atmosphere
attempt
audience
bachelor
bankrupt
barrel
barrelled
battalion
battery
bayonet
behaviour
beneficial
benzine
betroth
bilious
blamable
boisterous
bolder
boulder
brilliance
bulwark
bustling
campaign
capable
capital
catalogue
catastrophe
cavalier
cereal
changeable
chaos
choir
chloroform
chocolate
Christian
citizen
clayey
coercion
collapse

colliery
colossal
commandeer
commander
commemorate
commerce
commercial
comparative
competitor
complement
compliment
concrete
condemn
confectionery
confer
conferred
confiscate
connexion
conscience
conscientious
consequently
conspicuous
constitution
contemplate
contrary
control
controlled
conveyance
corps
corpse
correspondence
corridor
corrupt
countenance
counterfeit
courageous
crumbled
crumpled
cutlery

debris
deceive
depot
desert
dessert
design
dialogue
diameter
dilapidated
dinghy
dingy
disapproval
disaster
disastrous
disciple
discipline
disease
dispatch
dispel
dispelled
draft
draught
drudgery
duchess
duty
dutiful
efficiency
electricity
electrician
eligible
eloquent
emancipation
embezzle
embroidery
emergency
emigrate
emphasis
encouragement
engineer
ensue

ensuing
envelop
envelope
equal
equalled
equip
equipped
equipment
erroneous
exaggeration
excursion
experience
experiment
extraordinary
extravagance
extreme
fatal
fatally
fatigue
fatiguing
feign
fiery
forfeit
forlorn
formally
formerly
fortunately
freight
frivolous
frolic
frolicking
frolicsome
fulfil
fulfilled
fully
ful(l)ness
gamble
gambling
gambol　.
gambolling

garbage
garrison
gaudy
gauge
gauntlet
ghastly
glacier
glazier
gnarled
gorgeous
gorilla
guerilla
government
gramophone
grandeur
grievance
guarantee
guillotine
handkerchief
handsome
hansom
harass
heifer
hemisphere
hindrance
hoard
horde
human
humane
humour
humorous
hurricane
hygiene
hypocrisy
hypocrite
immovable
impassable
impetuous
implement
improvement

inconvenience
indebted
indigestible
ingredient
instantaneous
intellect
interpret
interpreted
intricacy
irritate
kerosene
khaki
knapsack
knell
laboratory
lattice
legible
leisure
liege
likelihood
liquefy
livelihood
lucerne
lullaby
luscious
magazine
magnify
magnificent
maintain
maintenance
maize
maze
management
martyr
marshal
martial
massacre
mechanical
medal
medallion

meddle
Mediterranean
melancholy
melody
melodious
meridian
methylated
mileage
minister
minster
miraculous
miscellaneous
mislaid
modify
monastery
monstrous
musician
museum
mutineers
nautical
necessarily
negligent
negotiation
noticeable
nucleus
nymph
obedience
obelisk
obstacle
occasional
occasionally
occurrence
ochre
odious
odorous
offensive
official
ointment
offence
omit

omitted
omission
oppressive
orchestra
ordinary
ordinarily
original
outrage
outrageous
overwhelm
oxygen
pacify
pageant
pamphlet
panic
panicky
pantomime
paraffin
paragraph
parallel
parliament
patrol
patrolled
pebbly
peculiar
peeling
peninsula (n)
perpendicular
persevere
perseverance
persistence
pessimist
petition
physician
picnic
picnicking
picturesque
pneumatic
pneumonia
political

politician
porpoise
portrait
precipice
precipitous
predecessor
prejudice
prevalent
principal
principle
privilege
programme
promontory
prophecy
prophesy
punctual
pyjamas
pyramid
quarrelsome
quays
queue
radish
realize
realm
recede
reducible
rehearse
rehearsal
renowned
repetition
reservoir
restaurant
retaliate
rheumatic
righteous
riotous
roguery
rustle
scaffold
sceptre

scourge
scrupulous
scythe
sepulchre
sergeant
sieve
siphon
sirloin
skeleton
smoulder
society
souvenir
sovereign
Spain
Spaniard
specialty
specimen
spectre
stalwart
stampede
stationary
stationery
statue
strenuous
stubborn
subsequent
suddenness
suicide
superstitious
surgeon
surveyor
sympathy
sympathetic
tarpaulin
tattoo
tattooed
telescope
temperament
temporary
temporarily

tenacity
tenacious
tendency
terrify
terrified
tragedy
transference
treachery
tributaries
triumph
truthful
turmoil
tyrant
tyranny
undoubtedly
unexpectedly
vacation
vaccination
vacuum
variety
ventilator
vicious
victuals
viscount
volunteer
wealthy
wealthiest
weird
welfare
whereabouts
whisky
wholesome
wilful
withhold
witnesses
wonderful
wondrous
worthy
worthiness
zephyr

14

SPELLING LIST FOR GRADE V (VICTORIA)

The following words are recommended by the Victorian Department of Education for study by pupils in Grade V, and for revision in Forms I and II.

(Reprinted by permission of the Victorian Department of Education.)

LIST A

accident	crowd	goal	platform
adventure	cupboard	guard	players
afterwards	dangerous	hadn't	possible
all right	decided	hobby	present
almost	different	horror	properly
already	dining	idea	really
although	direction	invited	received
amazed	distance	jewels	remembered
amongst	diving	joined	rescue
anywhere	easily	journey	reward
appeared	eighteen	listened	rifle
arrived	either	lonely	safely
attacked	eldest	machine	sandwiches
bathers	enemy	managed	scared
beautiful	enjoyed	meant	search
beauty	entered	meanwhile	several
believe	escape	mistress	shining
bicycle	everyone	motor	shoulder
biscuits	exciting	narrow	sign
buried	factory	native	somebody
burst	fairly	nearest	somewhere
cabin	farther	noticed	store
captured	fierce	office	straight
cause	fired	ourselves	study
centre	forced	palace	surprise
certain	forgotten	passage	taxi
clouds	form	passed	terrier
collecting	frightened	petrol	there's
concert	ghost	piano	thrown
couple	giant	pier	treasure

tunnel	village	witch	wrecked
umpire	wandered	wonderful	
veranda	whom	worry	
view	wireless	worth	

LIST B

action	crane	human	result
alight	creatures	important	rider
anchor	crocodile	instantly	roam
ankle	curtain	kookaburra	rubbish
arithmetic	dairy	lately	safety
arranged	delighted	length	scene
ashore	desert	lettuce	scent
autumn	diamond	level	servant
awakened	difficult	likely	service
bait	dismay	lorry	shallow
barley	district	lounge	shrubs
bathe	double	mare	silence
beneath	dreadful	merrily	simple
berries	expected	midday	smugglers
biting	explained	mirror	sneaked
blossom	fifth	murder	splendid
bounced	film	nature	startled
breath	gallop	neighbours	stretch
bullets	garage	nowhere	telephone
cafe	gear	offered	thieves
candle	golf	perfect	torch
caravan	groceries	photo	tough
carefully	handkerchief	plain	tour
cargo	handsome	playful	tractor
cellar	harbour	pleasure	treated
century	harness	plough	unknown
circle	haunted	powerful	useful
coco-nut	healthy	pretended	vain
coffee	heavily	prisoner	vase
company	herd	private	vegetables
content	higher	raid	voyage
courage	hired	refused	waist
craft	history	report	warning

weary	welcome	wharf	worn	written
weight	weren't	who's	wrapped	

LIST C

admiring	duty	mood	scolded
bacon	earlier	mosquitoes	screeching
banana	echo	murmured	sentence
beggar	engaged	mutton	serial
bough	equal	necklace	shepherd
brakes	express	obeyed	she's
breathe	fault	onions	shield
bridle	fortune	owing	sigh
brigade	fountain	pansies	signal
bruised	freedom	parade	speech
bugle	freezing	partner	spirit
camera	funniest	perch	squirrel
cast	geography	pity	steering
cell	glasses	poetry	strength
cement	glue	politely	suffering
clerk	grammar	pollard	surely
clumsy	grease	problem	switched
coarse	habit	produced	trembling
cocoa	harvest	pumpkin	trial
common	haul	pupils	trolley
companions	heaven	quarrel	trough
concrete	hero	rare	vessel
conductor	I'd	reef	victory
containing	insisted	remained	wardrobe
correct	jetty	remarked	wealthy
cough	kindergarten	removed	weapons
cushion	kindly	repair	weighed
damage	labour	ridden	western
defeated	lilies	ruined	whenever
defend	medal	rustle	woollen
dentist	mention	salad	you've
destroyed	merchant	sauce	
distant	metal	scarf	
divided	mistake	scissors	

SPELLING LIST FOR GRADE VI (VICTORIA)

The following words are recommended by the Victorian Department of Education for study by pupils in Grade VI, and for revision in Forms I and II.

(Reprinted by permission of the Victorian Department of Education.)

LIST A

aboard	curious	group	panic
aeroplane	decorated	height	parcel
allowed	dense	horrible	particular
aloud	destination	hospital	passengers
altogether	detective	hurriedly	patrol
amazement	disappeared	imagine	peaceful
ambulance	disappointed	impossible	period
ancient	discovered	including	pigeons
anxious	drifted	injured	pilot
approaching	electric	instance	pleasant
arrival	enormous	interesting	poison
astonished	entrance	introduced	popular
attention	equipment	investigate	position
awful	exactly	invitation	practice
bandage	excellent	jealous	practise
basin	exclaimed	laughter	prepared
beginning	exercise	library	puncture
boarding	explore	lightning	radio
carnival	explosion	luckily	rapidly
carriage	extra	luggage	recently
chaff	extremely	mainly	recovered
champion	famous	medicine	relations
channel	favourite	mischief	relief
chocolate	ferrets	modern	satisfied
cigarette	finally	museum	science
comfortable	forward	mystery	seized
completely	furniture	neither	serious
consisted	generally	occurred	settled
continued	gentleman	opposite	slippery
control	glorious	ordinary	special
court	gradually	oval	succeeded

success	term	thoroughly	valuable
suggested	terrible	tire (tyre)	various
suitable	terrific	travelling	visitors
supply	terrified	type	whether
surface	theatre	umbrella	you're
tennis	therefore	usually	

LIST B

acres	consent	inspector	provided
adult	convict	instructions	public
afford	coral	instrument	purpose
annoyed	costume	intended	required
area	current	interval	retired
arrested	curve	invisible	revealed
assistant	decent	item	revenge
attempted	defence	knowledge	revolver
attend	delivered	lagoon	section
average	described	lantern	selected
awarded	display	local	sense
balanced	disturbed	mane	separate
barrel	dreary	material	series
battery	drought	memory	skeleton
boring	eighth	messenger	soccer
boundary	engineer	miserable	solid
broad	event	mission	soul
bundle	examined	movement	sowing
bustle	example	musical	spaniel
cactus	fashion	nursery	submarine
canvas	fawn	obtained	sweat
carrier	female	occupied	telegram
ceased	ferry	octopus	telescope
ceiling	fever	orphan	they're
celebrated	fortunately	panel	threatened
characters	future	parlour	tomatoes
chemical	gallant	plaster	traffic
cockatoo	guilty	population	transport
collapse	happiness	poultry	tropical
collection	homestead	previous	uniform
college	honour	progress	unusual
composition	hurricane	proof	weir
condition	industry	property	

LIST C

abroad	connected	increased	quietened
absence	conquer	innocent	reasonable
according	construction	inquire	recess
account	continent	intelligent	region
ache	customs	issued	regular
active	debate	junction	remainder
address	debt	justice	repeated
admitted	declared	kiosk	request
advantage	degree	label	respect
altered	deny	laundry	retreat
amusement	departure	liquid	rhinoceros
annual	deserve	maize	route
appeal	desire	major	sandals
applied	disadvantage	marriage	securely
appointed	disgrace	mattress	seldom
armour	disgraceful	measles	sensible
aroused	disgusted	measured	settlement
assembly	dismiss	medical	shriek
attached	disobey	mineral	siren
author	distress	mining	standard
avenue	division	minister	statue
axle	doubt	miracle	strait
bargain	drawers	misfortune	style
barrier	duel	moisture	suburbs
benefit	education	monument	temperature
boomerang	effect	motion	title
boulder	encountered	mould	union
brief	encourage	national	urge
brooch	excuse	notion	vacant
canals	export	odour	veil
capable	farewell	pattern	violent
capital	fastened	pioneer	vision
chemist	florist	portion	volcano
citizens	frequently	prefer	volume
climate	fuel	presence	warriors
column	funeral	primary	width
compass	gorilla	profit	youth
complain	grateful	purchased	
composed	hoarse	quaint	
conclusion	importance	quality	

SPELLING LIST FOR FORM I (VICTORIA)

The following words are recommended by the Victorian Department of Education for study by pupils in Form I.

Average age of pupils in Form I is 12.6 years.
(Reprinted by permission of the Victorian Department of Education)

LIST A

aborigines
acid
adventurous
aerodrome
almond
ambition
angle
announced
apparatus
apparently
arena
arrangements
articles
artificial
attracted
audience
autograph
ballet
bewildered
brilliant
business
cabinet
cautiously
cavern
certificate
choir
chorus
christened

civilization
collided
commenced
committed
compartment
competition
confusion
considered
contact
conversation
corpse
council
delicate
delicious
depot
depth
description
determined
develop
dinghy
discussing
disguised
eerie
effort
energy
entirely
erected
especially

eventually
evidently
excitement
exhausted
exhibition
expedition
expensive
experience
experiments
glistening
gorgeous
government
guides
haversack
hockey
immediately
immensely
incident
information
intention
interrupted
junior
kerosene
kidnapped
laden
language
league
machinery

magazine
majesty
mansion
marvellous
mayor
mechanic
muscles
mysterious
naturally
necessary
nervous
niece
nuisance
numerous
occasionally
occupants
occupation
operation
opinion
opportunity
orchids
organized
orphanage
oxygen
parachute
patient

peculiar
permission
piercing
possession
practically
precious
preparations
probably
proceeded
professor
program[me
provisions
pyjamas
queue
radiator
realized
recognized
refreshments
relatives
released
relieved
sausages
scenery
schooner
senior
sheriff

similar
sincerely
situated
spacious
stealthily
stomach
submerged
successful
sufficient
supporters
surrounded
survived
suspicious
system
technical
throughout
tobacco
tremendous
truly
uncomfortable
university
ventured
weird
whilst
wreckage

LIST B

accompanied
accurate
accused
actual
admiration
admission

advanced
advertised
affair
affect
apartment
appearance

appetite
appointment
argument
artistic
assured
attendance

attraction
avail
awkward
behaviour
bungalow
Christian
civil
combination
command
commission
community
compared
concerned
conference
confidence
confident
continually
contrary
controlled
convince
courteous
decision
design
despair
destruction
diameter
disease
distinct
documents
domestic
dormitory
educational
entertainment
enthusiasm

envelope
essential
estate
evidence
exceedingly
explanation
expression
familiar
feature
fiction
generous
governor
hesitate
ignorant
impatient
impression
improvement
industrial
instructor
intelligence
interfere
international
interview
judg(e)ment
lawyer
liable
liberty
location
majority
medium
opera
original
paragraph
patience

performance
permanent
personal
photograph
possibility
president
principal
process
production
profession
profitable
quantities
reception
regularly
represent
resort
responsible
sacrifice
session
severe
situation
social
society
substance
suggestion
telegraph
temptation
territory
triumph
unnecessary
urgent
variety
victim
visible

SPELLING LIST FOR FORM II (VICTORIA)

Recommended by the Victorian Department of Education.

Average age of students is 13.6 years.

(Reprinted by permission of the Victorian Department of Education)

LIST A

actually
agony
album
alligator
ammunition
anxiety
approximately
ascend
association
atmosphere
attic
automatic
burglar
cannibals
career
cemetery
classical
commotion
confronted
consciousness
corridor
criminal

crystal
curiosity
curse
descended
dilapidated
disaster
draught
dynamite
electricity
enthusiastic
eucalyptus
extraordinary
foreign
gauge
guinea
gymnasium
gypsy
horizon
idol
inquisitive
irrigation
jewellery

laboratory
magnificent
manure
miniature
mischievous
monotonous
mountainous
persuaded
picturesque
plentiful
poisonous
procession
propeller
reluctantly
reservoir
secretary
sergeant
strenuous
torpedo
unconscious
unfortunately
vacation

LIST B

absolutely
accommodation
accomplished
accustomed
acquainted
activities
advertisement

advisable
agricultural
ambitious
anniversary
apologized
appreciate
appreciation

attitude
authority
available
banquet
beneficial
bureau
calendar

campaign
cashier
catalogue
characteristic
cheque
circular
circumstances
commercial
committee
comparison
conceived
confessed
congratulated
connexion
    (connection)
consequences
consequently
considerable
continuous
contrast
convenience
convenient
cordial
created
critical
cylinder
definitely
deposit
desperate
dispose
distinguished
distributed
dramatic
earnest
effective
efficient
elaborate
elected
elevator
emergency

enclosed
endeavour
estimated
exception
exceptionally
exchanged
executed
existence
expectation
exquisite
extensive
fascinating
freight
genius
guarantee
guardian
historical
imitation
inclined
individual
indulge
influence
inspiration
intensely
interior
leisure
licence (n.)
license (vb.)
liquor
literature
lodge
luncheon
mathematics
mechanical
military
minor
notified
obvious
opposition
orchestra

organization
perfection
perpetual
personality
physical
physician
pneumonia
positive
presentation
pressure
procure
professional
prosperous
reality
registered
recommendation
religious
representative
reputation
residence
respectable
respective
reverse
ridiculous
romantic
routine
sacred
scientific
stationary
stenographer
superintendent
superior
survey
theory
tragedy
transferred
vicinity
witness

SPELLING LIST FOR SENIOR YEARS

Department of Education recommendations have been included in this list.

abattoirs
abhorrence
abolition
abridgement
abscess
absorption
accelerate
accommodation
accumulate
acquiesce
acreage
adequate
admiralty
adolescent
advertisement
aesthetic
affiliation
amalgamate
amateur
ambassador
ambiguous
amelioration
amenable
amethyst
anaesthesia
analogous
analyst
anonymous
antithesis
apoplexy
apparel
apparition
arraign
assassinate
assessment
assuage
auctioneer

auxiliary
avoirdupois
banister
bankruptcy
barricade
biassed
bigoted
billiards
bivouac
bludgeon
bouquet
bronchitis
brusque
buoyant
burlesque
buttress
calibre
campaign
capricious
carburettor
caricature
cartilage
catarrh
centennial
champagne
chandelier
chimera
chrysanthemum
circuitous
coalesce
colleague
compatible
complaisant
conciliatory
connoisseur
constituency
consummate·

contumely
contumelious
convalescence
coquette
corroborate
credence
credentials
credulous
criticized
crystalline
dahlia
decadent
decrepit
deficiencies
deign
delicacy
delineate
demagogue
demeanour
desecrate
desiccated
deteriorate
diaphragm
diphtheria
diphthong
dishevel
dishevelled
dynasty
ecclesiastic
effervescent
eiderdown
embarrass
embodiment
encyclopaedia
enthusiastic
equanimity
equilibrium

etiquette
exchequer
excrescence
exhilarating
exuberant
fallacious
farcical
feign
filament
filial
flannelette
fortuitous
fuchsia
furlough
fury
furry
fusilier
gaiety
garrulous
gazette
gazetteer
genealogy
glycerine
gradient
granary
grievously
gullible
guttural
haemorrhage
harangue
hardihood
hearken
heinous
hereditary
heterogeneous
hierarchy
hieroglyphic
honorary
hydraulic
hypochondria

hysterical
idolatrous
ignominious
illegible
implacable
impropriety
impugn
incalculable
incendiary
inconceivable
incontrovertible
indefeasible
indefensible
indict
indisputable
ineffaceable
insatiable
insistent
instalment
instil
insurrection
intercede
interrogate
intrigue
inveigle
inveigh
irascible
iridescence
irreconcilable
irrelevant
irreparable
irresistible
irretrievable
isthmus
jealousy
jeopardy
judicial
justifiable
kaleidoscope
labyrinth

lacquer
leprous
lineament
longevity
loquacious
magnanimous
malicious
malleable
manageable
manoeuvre
masquerade
mattress
meagre
medicinal
mediocre
mercenary
mignonette
millennium
miniature
minstrelsy
misshapen
missile
misstatement
moccasin
morass
mortgage
mountaineer
moustache
munificence
myrrh
mythology
nasturtium
nauseous
negligible
neigh
obeisance
obligatory
obscene
obsequies
omelette

omniscient
openness
optician
origin
ostensible
pageantry
palisade
palliate
panegyric
paralysis
parenthesis
paroxysm
peaceable
peasantry
penitentiary
perceptible
perennial
perpetuity
perspicacity
phaeton
phenomenon
physician
physiognomy
piccaninny
piquant
plaintiff
plausible
plebeian
plebiscite
posthumous
practitioner
predicament
predilection
pre-eminent
preferable
preference
preferred
prejudice
presbytery
presumptuous

pretentious
privilege
profession
proficiency
pronounceable
proprietary
pseudonym
psychology
putrefy
quarrelled
quiescent
rarefy
rebellious
receptacle
reciprocity
reconnoitre
recurrence
reminiscence
rendezvous
reprehensible
reprieve
requital
resuscitate
revelation
reverie
rhapsody
rhythm
risible
riveter
sacrilege
saleable
sanctity
sanctuary
sanguinary
sapphire
sarsaparilla
satellite
scarify
scarlatina
sceptic

schedule
scintillate
separable
sepulchre
silhouetted
simultaneous
soliloquy
soliloquies
soliloquizes
specific
spontaneity
statistics
stateliness
strychnine
strategy
stupefy
subservience
subsidiary
subsidy
subterranean
subtle
subtlety
supercilious
superficial
superseded
suppression
surfeit
surpass
susceptible
sustenance
sycophant
symmetry
symmetrical
symphony
symptom
synagogue
synonymous
syringe
temporarily
terrific

tragedian
tranquillity
transcendent
transient
trousseau
truculent
ubiquitous
unanimous

unforgivable
unparalleled
unpronounceable
utilitarian
vacillate
variegated
vaseline
vermilion

vernacular
vicissitude
vilify
voluptuous
voracious
woollen
wreak

SPECIAL LISTS FOR SENIOR STUDENTS

The following lists were used in testing candidates for admission to teachers' colleges.

(Extract from "The Education Gazette")

SYDNEY COLLEGE LIST No. 1

monastery
vilify
dishevel
appal
plebeian
forbade
blamable
stupefy
luscious
corroborate
abattoirs
sacrilege
cemetery
icicle
scintillate
inaccessible
changeable
inveigh
scythe
chicory
jeopardy
siphon
chrysalis
accede
debris

arraign
reconnoitre
paraffin
battalion
riveter
canonical
haemorrhage
guttural
requital
cannibal
parricide
exhilarate
befall
biassed
farcical
piteous
recede
furlough
buoyant
Britannia
practicable
fulfilment
fuchsia
blissful
pleurisy

apparel
soluble
liquorice
colonnade
lacquer
skilful
collision
annotate
distil
moccasin
variegated
medallion
vacillate
desiccated
acquiesce
discreet
acreage
methylated
vaccinate
emissary
obeisance
ascetic
saccharine
hypocrisy
caterpillar

mattress
unparalleled
syringe
malleable
corollary
abscess
wholly
negotiate
embarrass

camellia
giddiness
accommodation
meagre
deign
underrate
edible
myrrh
worshipper

enrol
oscillate
banister
casualty
harass
rhythm
excel

SYDNEY COLLEGE LIST No. 2

duration
grammar
eloquence
acknowledged
assassination
extreme
appalling
business
embarrassment
deportment
possessive
inconvenience
society
consideration
extravagant
co-operated
petulant
information
distinction
implacable
colleague
shocking
rheumatic
woollen
preceding
imitate
remittances
circumstances

bitterness
accommodation
sovereign
parallel
ecstasy
recurrence
parliament
coefficient
secretary
irritable
execution
separate
uncomfortable
twelfth
quarrelled
irresistible
accustomed
analysis
vehement
similar
principal
heartily
occurrence
unconscious
supersede
practice (n)
attachment
beauteous

chorus
advice
conceived
eccentricity
excruciating
balance
audacious
hypotenuse
cheating
delinquents
disappoint
idolater
consolidate
governor
nucleus
development
judgement
February
expenses
manly
benefited
counterfeit
leisure
dilapidated
fearless
condemned

ARMIDALE COLLEGE LIST

expense	guard	ridiculous
accommodation	gauge	fulfilment
occasion	pastoral	origin
withhold	veins	adhere
separate	descent	professor
Britain	siege	allows
Mediterranean	wondrous	eminent
buried	pursue	indispensable
venomous	quite	acquiesce
privilege	believe	susceptible
valleys	ministry	elegy
edible	boundary	retaliate
paid	anointed	woollen
nominative	specimen	miniature
auxiliary	mountainous	melancholy
kangaroo	clothes	pantomime
strict	grammar	mentally
soluble	villain	innate
monastery	committee	superseded
tendency	superintendent	propeller
aqueduct	dissolve	freight
extension	poisonous	repetition
accessible	forty	heifer
swollen	devise	procedure
interfering	medicine	enrolment
omitted	existence	memento
occur	earthen	impostor
similarly	neuter	advise
install	imaginary	divine

ONE HUNDRED TROUBLESOME WORDS
GROUP 1

acreage	canoeing	forty
argument	dense	frolicked
bluish	dyeing	gaiety
bushel	ennoble	hoeing

loosen
mimicked
niece
paid
panicky
picnicking
piteous
separate

siege
sieve
similar
singeing
skilful
stony
swollen
truly

twelfth
weir
weird
wholly
wield
wilful
wiry
woolly

GROUP 2

barrenness
battalion
breathe
Britannia
development
drunkenness
enrol(ment)
exaggerate
favourite
fulfilment
gauge

honorary
honourable
humorous
humorist
inoculate
instalment
isosceles
liquefy
pavilion
persuade
pursue

putrefy
righteous
rottenness
similes
siphon
stubbornness
stupefy
tingeing
vigorous
yacht

GROUP 3

accommodation
acquiesce
anaesthetic
annihilate
antithesis
aqueduct
assassinate
chancellor
chloroform
colliery
colonnade

colossal
crystallize
desiccated
dissatisfied
ecstasy
embarrass
enthralment
harass
metallurgy
phlegm
psychology

reconnaissance
resuscitate
rhythm
sarsaparilla
strychnine
symmetry
tranquillity
unparalleled
vaccinate
vacillate

120 AMERICAN DEMONS

Constant testing in the 10,000 most commonly used words, as determined by the Commonwealth Investigation, revealed that the following words were most frequently misspelt in schools of eleven American States.

For class use they are divided into two groups.

GROUP 1

accommodation
accompanied
accrued
accumulate
achievement
acknowledgement
actuates
adequate
adieu
advantageous
affectionately
affiliated
all right
ammunition
anaesthetic
analyse
anniversary
anxiety
apologize
appreciative

awkward
bachelor
bankruptcy
bazaar
beneficial
beneficiary
bouquet
bronchitis
cemetery
chauffeur
Christian
column
committee
comparative
competition
conscience
conscientious
controversy
conveyance
counsel

countenance
criticism
curiosity
delinquent
descend
deterrent
discretion
dissatisfied
efficiency
eligible
eucalyptus
existence
exquisite
forfeiture
furlough
good-bye
guaranteed
hysterics
indefinitely
inferred

GROUP 2

insignia
intellectual
interpreted
interruption

irresistible
leisure
livelihood
maintenance

melancholy
miscellaneous
mischievous
morale

mortgage
murmur
museum
necessarily
negotiate
nuisance
omissions
ordinance
original
pamphlet
parallel
partial
patience
perceive
perseverance
phenomenon

physician
physiology
picturesque
prejudiced
privileged
procedure
profession
psychology
pursuing
questionnaire
refrigerator
remembrance
restaurant
rheumatic
schedule
seize

siege
solemn
sovereign
Spanish
specifically
statistics
surprise
tariff
temporarily
tragedy
transferred
undoubtedly
unnecessary
valuing
villain
walnut

ENGLISH LANGUAGE LIST

The following groups, compiled by experienced teachers, contain words which are in common use in various years.

GROUP 1

adjectival
adverbial
clause
colon
comma
composition
feminine

gender
grammar
masculine
neuter
nominative
objective
phrase

plural
poem
poetry
possessive
sentence
singular
speech

GROUP 2

analyse
analysis
author(ess)
character(istic)
conjunction
consonant
drama(tist)

literature
modify
novel(ist)
paragraph
predicate
preposition
principal

punctuation
qualify
quotation
style
subordinate
vocabulary
vowel

GROUP 3

auxiliary
comedy
comparative
comparison
comprehension
critic(ism)
dialogue

emphasis
exclamation
fiction(al)
history
historical
humour
humorous

interrogation
monologue
simile(s)
stanza(ic)
superlative
syllable
tragedy

GROUP 4

allusion
antonym
appropriate
ballad(ist)
biography
descriptive
exaggeration

explain
explanation
expression
lyric(al)
metaphor(ical)
metre
metrical

narrative
parable
participle
participial
rhyme
rhythm(ical)
synonym(ous)

GROUP 5

alliteration
ambiguity
apostrophe
apposition
classic(al)
climax
colloquial(ism)

diction
figurative
hyperbole
imperative
myth(ology)
paradox(ical)
paraphrase

personification
prosaic
repetition
satire
satirical
summarize
synopsis

GROUP 6

antithesis
caricature
didactic
elegy
epigram(matical)
euphony
hypallage

idyll(ic)
irony
metonymy
onomatopoeia
oxymoron
pamphlet
parenthesis

pentameter
pleonasm
quatrain
rhetoric(al)
soliloquy
sonnet(eer)
verbosity

WORDS WHICH MAY BE CONFOUNDED

Distinguish carefully between the following bracketed words in regard to meaning. Wherever possible, include the words in the same sentence: *e.g.*, From his castle tower the *baron* mournfully surveyed his *barren* fields.

GROUP 1

{ baron barren	{ altar alter	{ brim bream
{ to too two	{ gaol goal	{ border boarder
{ threw through	{ its it's	{ reel real

GROUP 2

{ quite quiet	{ peeling pealing	{ straight strait
{ story storey	{ sewing sowing	{ birth berth
{ peace piece	{ allowed aloud	{ brake break

GROUP 3

{ prophet profit	{ bury berry	{ bath bathe
{ bow bough	{ knightly nightly	{ saw seen
{ dairy diary	{ skull scull	{ singing singeing

GROUP 4

beach beech	need knead	fourth forth
freeze frieze	horde hoard	pail pale
pear pair pare	sore soar	vain vein vane

GROUP 5

creak creek	rest wrest	hair hare heir
maize maze	ark arc	bail bale
bell belle	lock loch	tired tied tide

GROUP 6

does doze dose	proceed precede	lose loose loss
navy navvy	accept except	addition edition
wet whet	weather whether wether	cloth clothe

GROUP 7

road rode rowed	their there they're	wholly holey holy

root	lend	course
rout	loan	coarse
route	lone	

| dying | sensible | glacier |
| dyeing | sensitive | glazier |

GROUP 8

| least | rung | wary |
| lest | wrung | weary |

minor	wrapped	alley
miner	rapped	ally
	rapt	

| past | counsel | presence |
| passed | council | presents |

GROUP 9

lied	flowed	gallon
lay	flown	galleon
laid	fled	

hung	sight	colonel
hanged	site	kernel
	cite	

| desert | airy | wait |
| dessert | eyrie | weight |

GROUP 10

right	gentle	bark
rite	genteel	barque
write		

| practice | advice | loving |
| practise | advise | lovable |

| mantle | cast | faint |
| mantel | caste | feint |

GROUP 11

| gate | cask | waste |
| gait | casque | waist |

| born | gage | poplar |
| borne | gauge | popular |

| sole | did | yolk |
| soul | done | yoke |

GROUP 12

| mourning | serial | dragon |
| morning | cereal | dragoon |

		corps
pier	isle	corpse
peer	aisle	copse

| guild | check | quarts |
| gild | cheque | quartz |

GROUP 13

| scurfy | stationary | carrot |
| scurvy | stationery | carat |

		idol
gorilla	gamble	idle
guerilla	gambol	idyll

| receipt | currant | draft |
| recipe | current | draught |

GROUP 14

| metal | device | councillor |
| mettle | devise | counsellor |

raise rise	discover invent	aught ought
licence license	moral morale	wave waive

GROUP 15

amount number	exceed accede	extent extant
libel slander	correspondence correspondents	meter metre
brooch broach	canvas canvass	recent resent

GROUP 16

affect effect	decease disease	surplice surplus
decent dissent descent	sear seer	minister minster
eligible illegible	slow slough	populace populous

GROUP 17

pouring poring	censer censor censure	cymbal symbol
statue stature statute	principal principle	bazaar bizarre
fatal fateful	stalactite stalagmite	gristly grisly grizzly

GROUP 18

deficient
defective

human
humane

eminent
imminent

perpetrate
perpetuate

physic
physique

courtesy
curtsy

afflict
inflict

credible
credulous
creditable

lighting
lightning
lightening

civility
servility

auger
augur

prophecy
prophesy

GROUP 19

perspective
prospective

continual
continuous

confer
defer
refer
infer

mysterious
mystical

tactful
tactical

stimulus
stimulant

adverse
averse

childish
childlike

incredible
incredulous

astrology
astronomy

compliment
complemen

antic
antique

GROUP 20

forego
forgo

expedient
expeditious

detract
distract

demur
demure

depreciate
deprecate

constancy
consistency

potent
potential

precipitate
precipitous

imperial
imperious

noticeable
notable
notorious

emigrant
immigrant

luxuriant
luxurious

GROUP 21

{ officious
{ official

{ satire
{ satyr

{ obedience
{ obeisance

{ elicit
{ illicit
{ solicit

{ ingenious
{ ingenuous

{ efficient
{ effective
{ effectual
{ efficacious

{ verbal
{ verbose

{ appreciable
{ appreciative

{ ordinance
{ ordnance

{ equable
{ equitable

{ formerly
{ formally

{ liniment
{ lineament

GROUP 22

{ temporary
{ temporal

{ essay
{ assay

{ transient
{ transitive
{ transitional

{ errand
{ errant
{ arrant

{ beneficent
{ benevolent

{ complacent
{ complaisant

{ difference
{ deference

{ allusion
{ illusion
{ delusion

{ impertinent
{ impenitent

{ ascetic
{ acetic
{ aesthetic

{ opposite
{ apposite

{ difficulty
{ dilemma

GROUP 23

{ literally
{ practically
{ virtually

{ punctual
{ punctilious

{ invaluable
{ valueless

{ salutary
{ salubrious

{ intense
{ intensive

{ tacit
{ taciturn

{ ostensible
{ ostentatious

{ urban
{ urbane

{ construct
{ construe

{ distinct
{ distinctive

{ superficial
{ supercilious

{ imaginary
{ imaginative

GROUP 24

{ contagious
{ contiguous

{ venal
{ venial

{ plaintive
{ plaintiff

{ accessory
{ accessary

{ contemptuous
{ contemptible

{ implicit
{ explicit

{ judicial
{ judicious

{ corporal
{ corporeal

{ depository
{ depositary

{ perspicacity
{ perspicuity

{ critic
{ critique

{ triumphal
{ triumphant

ADJECTIVES AND THEIR OPPOSITES

The following groups are designed to extend vocabulary and to test spelling ability. The adjectives of each group should be read to the students, who will then write the appropriate negative adjectives.

GROUP 1

accurate	inaccurate	necessary	unnecessary
active	inactive	patient	impatient
attentive	inattentive	perfect	imperfect
capable	incapable	pleasant	unpleasant
certain	uncertain	popular	unpopular
competent	incompetent	possible	impossible
honest	dishonest	probable	improbable
legal	illegal	pure	impure
loyal	disloyal	selfish	unselfish
mortal	immortal	visible	invisible

GROUP 2

agreeable	disagreeable
contented	discontented
convenient	inconvenient
definite	indefinite
dependent	independent
distinct	indistinct
equal	unequal
experienced	inexperienced
fortunate	unfortunate
healthy	unhealthy
honourable	dishonourable
limitable	illimitable
movable	immovable
polite	impolite
resistible	irresistible
resolute	irresolute
responsible	irresponsible
satisfied	dissatisfied
truthful	untruthful
worthy	unworthy

GROUP 3

accessible	inaccessible
conscious	unconscious
considerate	inconsiderate
constant	inconstant
courteous	discourteous
digestible	indigestible
eligible	ineligible
frequent	infrequent
legitimate	illegitimate
mobile	immobile
natural	unnatural
orderly	disorderly
partial	impartial
passable	impassable
penetrable	impenetrable
recoverable	irrecoverable
religious	irreligious
respectful	disrespectful
similar	dissimilar
wary	unwary

GROUP 4

adequate	inadequate
advantageous	disadvantageous
animate	inanimate
clement	inclement
constitutional	unconstitutional
credible	incredible
creditable	discreditable
controllable	uncontrollable
earthly	unearthly
grammatical	ungrammatical

limited	unlimited
logical	illogical
moderate	immoderate
pious	impious
prudent	imprudent
relevant	irrelevant
repressible	irrepressible
reputable	disreputable
separable	inseparable
timely	untimely

NOUNS AND THEIR ADJECTIVES

Here follow eight groups designed to extend vocabulary and to test spelling ability. The nouns should be read to the students, who will be required to write the appropriate adjectives

GROUP 1   GROUP 2

beauty	beautiful	adventure	adventurous
caution	cautious	cloud	cloudy
compulsion	compulsory	colony	colonial
coward	cowardly	despair	desperate
cyclone	cyclonic	four	fourth
danger	dangerous	fury	furious
deceit	deceitful	giant	gigantic
defiance	defiant	marvel	marvellous
disaster	disastrous	melody	melodious
dwarf	dwarfish	monster	monstrous
friend	friendly	order	orderly
glass	glassy	rain	rainy
guilt	guilty	religion	religious
grass	grassy	shade	shady
hunger	hungry	twelve	twelfth
knight	knightly	villain	villainous
leaf	leafy	venom	venomous
number	numerous	wealth	wealthy
peace	peaceful	winter	wintry
pebble	pebbly	wool	woollen

GROUP 3

advantage	advantageous	frost	frosty
aristocrat	aristocratic	glue	gluey
bounty	bountiful	gold	golden
chaos	chaotic	haste	hasty
chivalry	chivalrous	humour	humorous
conceit	conceited	lustre	lustrous
courage	courageous	scandal	scandalous
discontent	discontented	show	showy
excess	excessive	sponge	spongy
fop	foppish	success	successful

GROUP 4

choir	choral
clamour	clamorous
conscience	conscientious
contagion	contagious
empire	imperial
haze	hazy
hypocrite	hypocritical
labour	laborious
lethargy	lethargic
majesty	majestic
manor	manorial
merit	meritorious
metal	metallic
myth	mythical
origin	original
panic	panicky
pathos	pathetic
precipice	precipitous
republic	republican
traitor	traitorous

GROUP 5

angle	angular
apology	apologetic
avarice	avaricious
capacity	capacious
crystal	crystalline
custom	customary
defect	defective
finance	financial
glamour	glamorous
glutton	gluttonous
influence	influential
lucre	lucrative
miracle	miraculous
option	optional
regiment	regimental
rogue	roguish
science	scientific
suicide	suicidal
system	systematic
vigour	vigorous

GROUP 6

calamity	calamitous
caprice	capricious
culture	cultural
devotion	devotional
egoist	egoistic
hysteria	hysterical
legend	legendary
libel	libellous
luxury	luxurious
omen	ominous

pestilence	pestilential
reminiscence	reminiscent
rhythm	rhythmic
sedition	seditious
spasm	spasmodic
symbol	symbolic
territory	territorial
tumult	tumultuous
volume	voluminous
wasp	waspish

GROUP 7

circumstance	circumstantial
contumely	contumelious
delirium	delirious
democrat	democratic
emotion	emotional

epilepsy	epileptic
example	exemplary
heir	hereditary
ignominy	ignominious
odour	odorous

palace	palatial	result	resultant
panorama	panoramic	sacrifice	sacrificial
paradox	paradoxical	shrew	shrewish
phlegm	phlegmatic	sympathy	sympathetic
rancour	rancorous	unction	unctuous

GROUP 8

clergy	clerical	opprobrium	opprobrious
dyspepsia	dyspeptic	orchestra	orchestral
ecstasy	ecstatic	paralysis	paralytic
fragment	fragmentary	parsimony	parsimonious
medicine	medicinal	period	periodic
minister	ministerial	prejudice	prejudicial
monastery	monastic	spleen	splenetic
music	musical	supplement	supplementary
necessity	necessitous	symmetry	symmetrical
odium	odious	triumph	triumphal

VERBS AND THEIR NOUNS

The following six groups should be treated in the same manner as NOUNS AND THEIR ADJECTIVES. Make sure that you can spell both verbs and nouns.

GROUP 1

admit	admission	equip	equipment
appear	appearance	explode	explosion
argue	argument	extend	extension
collide	collision	fly	flight
confess	confession	navigate	navigation
conquer	conquest	propose	proposal
decide	decision	pursue	pursuit
describe	description	seize	seizure
discover	discovery	select	selection
elect	election	withdraw	withdrawal

GROUP 2

		GROUP 3	
advertise	advertisement	applaud	applause
apply	application	approve	approval
consume	consumption	calculate	calculation
cultivate	cultivation	communicate	communication
deceive	deceit	create	creation
defy	defiance	deport	deportation
deny	denial	descend	descent
destroy	destruction	distribute	distribution
disobey	disobedience	elope	elopement
dominate	domination	evade	evasion
enter	entry	flatter	flattery
expel	expulsion	incline	inclination
exclaim	exclamation	include	inclusion
explain	explanation	isolate	isolation
inquire	inquiry	omit	omission
judge	judgement	proclaim	proclamation
marry	marriage	reduce	reduction
persecute	persecution	reproduce	reproduction
solve	solution	succeed	succession
submit	submission	supervise	supervision

GROUP 4

acclaim	acclamation	divert	diversion
acquire	acquisition	dote	dotage
allude	allusion	fulfil	fulfilment
analyse	analysis	interpret	interpretation
anticipate	anticipation	mispronounce	mispronunciation
betroth	betrothal	persuade	persuasion
cancel	cancellation	recognize	recognition
depend	dependence	subscribe	subscription
detain	detention	transmit	transmission
discolour	discolo(u)ration	verify	verification

GROUP 5

abolish	abolition	coalesce	coalition
acknowledge	acknowledgement	corrode	corrosion
acquit	acquittal	denounce	denunciation
adore	adoration	deprive	deprivation
assail	assault	diminish	diminution

dispossess	dispossession	generate	generation
dissent	dissension	modify	modification
dissuade	dissuasion	notify	notification
encumber	encumbrance	perceive	perception
entreat	entreaty	protrude	protrusion

GROUP 6

abound	abundance	embezzle	embezzlement
abstain	abstinence	forfeit	forfeiture
accumulate	accumulation	impeach	impeachment
cajole	cajolery	presume	presumption
coerce	coercion	prevail	prevalence
corroborate	corroboration	renounce	renunciation
disavow	disavowal	renovate	renovation
efface	effacement	resume	resumption
effervesce	effervescence	reveal	revelation
elide	elision	transpose	transposition

VOCABULARY EXPANSION EXERCISES: NOUNS AND THEIR ADJECTIVES

Write the following nouns and place opposite each its corresponding adjective.

Group 1	Group 2	Group 3
accident	atom	ambition
acrobat	brilliance	drama
athlete	centre	dread
boy	child	eloquence
dust	crime	heathen
faith	duty	heaven
fault	fiend	history
filth	fragrance	hygiene
grace	friend	logic
greed	gloom	nation
industry	glory	optimism
innocence	gust	pain
insolence	impudence	plenty
mud	intelligence	shame
night	mercy	sorrow
patriot	pride	splendour
poison	quiet	storm
silver	sarcasm	treachery
wit	tragedy	victory
youth	violence	waste

GROUP 4	GROUP 5	GROUP 6
alcohol	ambiguity	abhorrence
cylinder	benevolence	ancestry
democracy	character	apathy
despot	cynic	autocrat
event	emphasis	choler
gore	fanatic	circuit
graph	frolic	discord
horizon	gas	hazard
idiot	idiom	hypnosis
lenience	imp	idyll
majesty	moral	indolence
pity	nomad	irony
poetry	pessimism	metaphor
scene	piety	remedy
theory	preference	satire
thunder	riot	strategy
virtue	sentiment	synonym
voice	tyranny	tact
volcano	vigil	vehicle
wile	vivacity	vision

VERBS AND THEIR NOUNS

Write the following verbs and place opposite each its corresponding noun.

GROUP 1	GROUP 2	GROUP 3
ascend	command	accuse
behave	correct	acquaint
bury	contest	adopt
carry	cure	astonish
combine	depart	burgle
delay	disqualify	celebrate
discuss	employ	concentrate
donate	enrol	decrease
engage	entertain	encourage
inspect	evaporate	fascinate
interfere	glare	glow
interrupt	irrigate	inspire
occupy	postpone	interject

operate	recover	perform
rehearse	resemble	pronounce
remove	retire	prosecute
roar	revenge	recite
struggle	rustle	remember
suffocate	slave	ventilate
torment	surprise	whisper

GROUP 4	GROUP 5	GROUP 6
abbreviate	accent	babble
abdicate	achieve	betray
advance	agitate	butcher
compose	bombard	delete
declare	elevate	demolish
develop	embarrass	devastate
enchant	enclose	deviate
establish	erode	distort
fumigate	erupt	encroach
gleam	exaggerate	endorse
grasp	exempt	fortify
immigrate	exterminate	humiliate
inhale	impede	inoculate
inject	liberate	insert
inscribe	penetrate	insinuate
obstruct	persist	intervene
persevere	proceed	ordain
prove	rout	perplex
question	stampede	rescind
relieve	utter	taint

ADJECTIVES AND THEIR NOUNS

Write the following adjectives and place opposite each its corresponding noun.

GROUP 1	GROUP 2	GROUP 3
active	anxious	agile
bald	blind	brutal
brave	certain	dense
cruel	clear	drowsy
curious	cunning	eager
daring	dim	fierce
dark	dizzy	final
difficult	hostile	indignant

evil	jealous	just
gentle	lazy	lonely
happy	loyal	moist
honest	popular	neutral
merry	punctual	quiet
pure	ready	rowdy
rude	strange	scarce
safe	strong	simple
stern	timid	solemn
strict	vulgar	stubborn
true	wide	superior
wise	wild	visible

GROUP 4	GROUP 5	GROUP 6
absurd	acute	austere
awkward	brief	authentic
divine	eccentric	deft
dreary	entire	desolate
earnest	eternal	didactic
harsh	expert	discreet
hoarse	fickle	frail
lively	futile	gay
nice	gallant	grand
obscure	inhuman	ingenious
peculiar	noble	lax
perfect	private	likely
savage	rank	moderate
severe	rapid	moody
similar	robust	obstinate
sincere	secret	resolute
solid	secure	stately
sudden	sober	sublime
tender	tense	subtle
virile	tranquil	supreme

VERBS, NOUNS AND ADJECTIVES

Look at the following table:

VERB	NOUN	ADJECTIVE
educate	education	educational
extend	extension	extensive

Draw a similar table, and put each word in the following groups in its correct place. Then, as required, add the two corresponding words.

GROUP 1

attend (vb)	love (vb)	speed (vb)
difference (n.)	obedient (adj.)	studious (adj.)
excite (vb)	quarrel (n.)	talk (n.)
fear (n.)	ridicule (vb)	taste (vb)
grease (n.)	risk (n.)	weary (adj.)
hope (vb)	sharp (adj.)	wonder (vb)
idle (adj.)	sleep (n.)	

GROUP 2

anger (n.)	free (adj.)	repress (vb)
bump (vb)	honour (n.)	satisfy (vb)
calm (adj.)	imagine (vb)	silent (adj.)
comfort (vb)	irritate (vb)	smoke (n.)
contradiction (n.)	neglect (n.)	steal (vb)
enjoy (vb)	pleasant (adj.)	value (n.)
foolish (adj.)	rebel (vb)	

GROUP 3

abuse (n.)	hate (vb)	profit (n.)
consider (vb)	indicate (vb)	protect (vb)
deep (adj.)	infection (n.)	separate (adj.)
defend (vb)	injurious (adj.)	stiff (adj.)
delight (n.)	murder (n.)	suspect (vb)
disgrace (n.)	possess (vb)	vacant (adj.)
excellent (adj.)	produce (vb)	

GROUP 4

advice (n.)	equal (adj.)	master (vb)
agree (vb)	expand (vb)	offence (n.)
attractive (adj.)	expense (n.)	oppress (vb)
complement (n.)	fertile (adj.)	regret (n.)

danger (n.)   grieve (vb)   suffice (vb)
desire (vb)   invention (n.)   watch (n.)
envy (vb)   mad (adj.)

GROUP 5

conclude (vb)   perfect (adj.)   respect (n.)
co-operation (n.)   prohibit (vb)   retain (vb)
economical (adj.)   provocation (n.)   romantic (adj.)
insist (vb)   recur (vb)   stupid (adj.)
introduce (vb)   reflect (vb)   trouble (n.)
migrate (vb)   reliant (adj.)   vex (vb)
mutiny (n.)   repent (vb)

GROUP 6

appreciate (vb)   loose (adj.)   revere (vb)
assert (vb)   observe (vb)   ruinous (adj.)
blaspheme (vb)   preparation (n.)   submit (vb)
congratulation (n.) prevail (vb)   toleration (n.)
harmony (n.)   prophecy (n.)   tough (adj.)
imitative (adj.)   prosperous (adj.)   vary (vb)
inform (vb)   response (n.)

PLURALS OF NOUNS

Most nouns form their plurals by adding "—s" to the
singular: *boy, boys*.

Plural in —ES

SINGULAR	PLURAL	SINGULAR	PLURAL
alias	aliases	marsh	marshes
box	boxes	speech	speeches
gas	gases	surplus	surpluses
lass	lasses	waltz	waltzes

Nouns ending in —Y

SINGULAR	PLURAL	SINGULAR	PLURAL
alley	alleys	journey	journeys
ally	allies	kidney	kidneys
city	cities	lily	lilies
comedy	comedies	mercy	mercies
fly	flies	monkey	monkeys

SINGULAR	PLURAL	SINGULAR	PLURAL
quantity	quantities	tragedy	tragedies
sky	skies	trolley	trolleys
storey	storeys	turkey	turkeys
story	stories	valley	valleys
sty	sties	volley	volleys

Nouns ending in —O

GROUP 1

SINGULAR	PLURAL	SINGULAR	PLURAL
bamboo	bamboos	mango	mangoes
banjo	banjos	merino	merinos
buffalo	buffaloes	mosquito	mosquitoes
calico	calicoes	motto	mottoes
cargo	cargoes	negro	negroes
curio	curios	no	noes
dingo	dingoes	piano	pianos
domino	dominoes	potato	potatoes
echo	echoes	silo	silos
grotto	grottoes	studio	studios
halo	haloes	tobacco	tobaccos
hero	heroes	tomato	tomatoes

GROUP 2

SINGULAR	PLURAL	SINGULAR	PLURAL
archipelago	archipelagos	fresco	frescos
desperado	desperadoes	ghetto	ghettos
dynamo	dynamos	inferno	infernos
embargo	embargoes	innuendo	innuendoes
embryo	embryos	magneto	magnetos
fiasco	fiascos	major-domo	major-domos

SINGULAR	PLURAL	SINGULAR	PLURAL
manifesto	manifestos	stiletto	stilettos
memento	mementos	tornado	tornadoes
portfolio	portfolios	torpedo	torpedoes
portico	porticos	torso	torsos
proviso	provisos	veto	vetoes
ratio	ratios	volcano	volcanoes

Irregular Plurals

SINGULAR	PLURAL	SINGULAR	PLURAL
calf	calves	mongoose	mongooses
child	children	oaf	oafs or oaves
elf	elves	ox	oxen
goose	geese	scarf	scarfs or scarves
hoof	hoofs or hooves	sheaf	sheaves
half	halves	shelf	shelves
knife	knives	thief	thieves
leaf	leaves	wharf	wharfs or wharves
life	lives	wife	wives
loaf	loaves	wolf	wolves
louse	lice		

Plurals of Compound Nouns

SINGULAR	PLURAL
aide-de-camp	aides-de-camp
armful	armfuls (cupfuls, handfuls, etc.)
*attorney general	attorneys general
brother-in-law	brothers-in-law (mothers-in-law, etc.)
*court martial	courts martial
commander-in-chief	commanders-in-chief
knight-errant	knights-errant
†lieutenant general	lieutenant generals

SINGULAR	PLURAL
†major general	major generals
man-eater	man-eaters
man-of-war	men-of-war
manservant	menservants
member of parliament	members of parliament
*postmaster general	postmasters general

*Expressions of this type (noun followed by adjective) require no hyphen except in the possessive case. The hyphen is also employed in *court martial* when the expression is used as a verb.

†Written as two words when used as an independent noun, but when used as a prefix the hyphen is inserted: *Major-General Smith.*

Foreign Plurals

GROUP 1

SINGULAR	PLURAL	SINGULAR	PLURAL
analysis	analyses	larva	larvae
apex	*apices *or* apexes	oasis	oases
aphis	aphides	octopus	octopuses
axis	axes	plateau	plateaux (*or* -s)
basis	bases	radius	radii
beau	beaux	stimulus	stimuli
crisis	crises	syllabus	syllabi (*or* -buses)
curriculum	curricula	tableau	tableaux
formula	formulae (*or* -s)	terminus	termini (*or* -uses)
fungus	fungi (*or* -uses)	vacuum	vacua *or* vacuums
hippopotamus	hippopotamuses	vertex	vertices* *or* vertexes

*The tendency is to keep *-ices* for scientific and formal contexts.

Foreign Plurals

GROUP 2

SINGULAR	PLURAL	SINGULAR	PLURAL
addendum	addenda	honorarium	-ia *or* -iums
antithesis	antitheses	hypothesis	hypotheses
automaton	automata (*or* -s)	memorandum	memoranda
calyx	calyces *or* calyxes	nucleus	nuclei
chrysalis	chrysalises	parenthesis	parentheses
criterion	criteria	phenomenon	phenomena
dictum	dicta *or* dictums	spectrum	spectra
dogma	dogmas	stratum	strata
ellipsis	ellipses	synopsis	synopses
erratum	errata	synthesis	syntheses
focus	focuses *or* foci	thesis	theses
genus	genera	ultimatum	ultimatums *or* ultimata

Plurals Same As Singular

chassis	grouse	series
*corps	innings	sheep
counsel (advocate)	reindeer	species
deer	salmon	trout

*The singular is pronounced *kor;* the plural *korz.*

Two Plurals With Different Meanings

SINGULAR	PLURAL	PLURAL
brother	brothers *(of the same family)*	brethren *(of the same society)*
cloth	cloths *(kinds of cloth)*	clothes *(garments)*
die	dies *(stamps for coining, etc.)*	dice *(cubes for games)*
fish	fish *(quantity)*	fishes *(number)*
genius	geniuses *(men of great talent)*	genii *(spirits)*
index	indexes *(tables of contents)*	indices *(algebraic exponents)*
penny	pence *(a sum)*	pennies *(separate coins)*
shot	shot *(little balls)*	shots *(discharges)*

Exercises

Give the plurals of the following nouns:

GROUP 1

business	council	kiss	pocketful
cast	country	lady	porpoise
chimney	dwarf	mattress	reef
church	fox	mouse	roof
committee	gallery	mouth	strife
conqueror	gulf	pasty	tooth

GROUP 2

bandit	larva	platypus	soliloquy
base	lord justice	princess royal	sphinx
bureau	Maori	rhinoceros	suffix
cherub	matinee	sergeant major	stigma
contralto	medium	simile	vortex
fife	menu	solicitor general	will-o'-the-wisp

GENDERS OF NOUNS

MASCULINE	FEMININE	MASCULINE	FEMININE
abbot	abbess	gander	goose
actor	actress	gentleman	lady
adventurer	adventuress	giant	giantess
bachelor	maid, spinster	god	goddess
baron	baroness	hart	roe
beau	belle	heir	heiress
benefactor	benefactress	hero	heroine
boar	sow	horse	mare
bridegroom	bride	horseman	horsewoman
buck	doe	host	hostess
bull	cow	hunter	huntress
canon	canoness	husband	wife
cock	hen	king	queen
cockerel	pullet	lad	lass
cock-sparrow	hen-sparrow	landlord	landlady
colt	filly	lion	lioness
count	countess	lord	lady
czar	czarina	manservant	maidservant
dauphin	dauphiness	marquis	marchioness
dog	bitch	master	mistress
drake	duck	mayor	mayoress
duke	duchess	monk, friar	nun
earl	countess	negro	negress
emperor	empress	nephew	niece
executor	executrix	peacock	peahen
father	mother	peer	peeress
priest	priestess	stallion	mare
prophet	prophetess	steer	heifer
proprietor	proprietress	steward	stewardess
ram	ewe	sultan	sultana
shepherd	shepherdess	traitor	traitress
sire (horse)	dam	uncle	aunt
son	daughter	viscount	viscountess
songster	songstress	waiter	waitress
sorcerer	sorceress	widower	widow
stag	hind	wizard	witch

RULES FOR THE POSSESSIVE

1. The possessive singular of nouns is formed by adding the apostrophe and "s" ('s).
Example: Addison's essays.
Jones's store.

Exception:
Where the addition of a hissing sound to words of two or more syllables is disagreeable to the ear, the apostrophe alone (') is used.
Examples: Moses' law.
Conscience' sake.

2. The possessive plural of nouns is formed by:
   (a) Adding the apostrophe alone (') to nouns ending in "s."
   Examples: Boys' school.
   Teachers' college.
   (b) Adding the apostrophe and "s" ('s) to nouns which do not have a plural ending in "s."
   Examples: Women's frocks.
   Men's suits.

3. The possessive of nouns in apposition is obtained by forming the possessive on the second noun only.
Example: Charles, the King's, defeat by the followers of Cromwell. . .

4. Common possession by several nouns is obtained by forming the possessive of the last noun.
Example England, America and Russia's efforts . . .

5. The possessive of compound nouns is obtained by forming the possessive on the last part.
Example· Brother-in-law's home.

Note.—If the compound word is plural, the possessive is still formed on the last part.
Example Brothers-in-law's homes.

6. Personal pronouns do not employ the apostrophe to form the possessive.
Example: Its tail.

Note.—"It's" is an abbreviation of "it is".

VERBS AND THEIR PRINCIPAL PARTS

The present indicative (1st person singular), the past indicative (1st person singular), and the past participle are called the "principal parts" of a verb.

Variations are so numerous that the correct forms can be learnt only by observation.

Verbs and their parts, which frequently cause difficulty, are listed below. Forms rarely used at the present day are placed in brackets.

VERBS AND THEIR PRINCIPAL PARTS

Present Indicative 1st person singular	Past Indicative 1st person singular	Past Participle
am	was	been
arise	arose	arisen
awake	awoke	awaked
bear	bore	borne
beat	beat	beaten
become	became	become
begin	began	begun
behold	beheld	beheld
bend	bent	bent
bid	bad, bade, bid	bidden, bid
bite	bit	bitten (bit)
bleed	bled	bled
blow	blew	blown
break	broke	broken
breed	bred	bred
build	built	built
burst	burst	burst
buy	bought	bought
cast	cast	cast
catch	caught	caught
choose	chose	chosen
cling	clung	clung
clothe	clothed, clad	clothed, clad
creep	crept	crept
crow	crew, crowed	crowed
deal	dealt	dealt

Present Indicative 1st person singular	Past Indicative 1st person singular	Past Participle
dig	dug	dug
do	did	done
draw	drew	drawn
dream	dreamt, dreamed	dreamt, dreamed
drink	drank	drunk
drive	drove	driven
dwell	dwelt	dwelt
eat	ate	eaten
fall	fell	fallen
flee	fled	fled
fling	flung	flung
flow	flowed	flowed
fly	flew	flown
forbid	forbade	forbidden
forgive	forgave	forgiven
freeze	froze	frozen
give	gave	given
grow	grew	grown
hang	hung, hanged*	hung, hanged*
hear	heard	heard
hew	hewed	hewn, hewed
hide	hid	hidden, hid
kneel	knelt	knelt
knit	knitted, knit	knitted, knit
know	knew	known
lay	laid	laid
lead	led	led
lend	lent	lent
lie	lay	lain (to recline)
lie	lied	lied (to speak falsely)
light	lit, lighted	lit, lighted
lose	lost	lost
mean	meant	meant
melt	melted	melted
mow	mowed	mown, mowed
pay	paid	paid

*Used only in the sense of "executed by hanging".

Present Indicative 1st person singular	Past Indicative 1st person singular	Past Participle
prove	proved	proved
raise	raised	raised
read	read	read
rend	rent	rent
rid	ridded, rid	rid (ridded)
ride	rode	ridden
ring	rang	rung
rise	rose	risen
saw	sawed	sawn
say	said	said
see	saw	seen
seek	sought	sought
sell	sold	sold
sew	sewed	sewn, sewed
shake	shook	shaken
shear	sheared (shore)	shorn (sheared)
shed	shed	shed
shine	shone	shone
shoe	shod	shod
shoot	shot	shot
show	showed	shown
shrink	shrank	shrunk
sing	sang	sung
slay	slew	slain
sleep	slept	slept
slide	slid	slid
sling	slung	slung
smell	smelt (smelled)	smelt (smelled)
smite	smote	smitten
sow	sowed	sown, sowed
speed	sped	sped
spell	spelt, spelled	spelt, spelled
spin	spun, span	spun
spoil	spoilt, spoiled	spoilt, spoiled
spring	sprang	sprung
steal	stole	stolen
stick	stuck	stuck
sting	stung	stung

Present Indicative 1st person singular	Past Indicative 1st person singular	Past Participle
strew	strewed	strewn, strewed
strive	strove	striven
swear	swore	sworn
sweep	swept	swept
swell	swelled	swollen, swelled
swim	swam	swum
swing	swung	swung
take	took	taken
teach	taught	taught
tear	tore	torn
throw	threw	thrown
tread	trod	trodden, trod
wake	woke, waked	waked, woken, woke
wear	wore	worn
weave	wove	woven
weep	wept	wept
wind	wound	wound
wring	wrung	wrung
write	wrote	written

PREPOSITIONAL IDIOMS

Certain verbs, nouns and adjectives are followed by particular prepositions. While the following represent commonly adopted usage, they must not be accepted without question: shades of meaning may, in some cases, require the use of other prepositions.

GROUP 1

They were ACCUSED *of* the crime.
The farm is ADJACENT *to* the railway station.
I AGREED *with* him *on* the question.
Did they APOLOGIZE *to* you *for* their conduct?
The peasants APPEALED *to* their lord *for* assistance.
I believe that he is CAPABLE *of* great bravery.

Are you CONFIDENT *of* success?
The general expressed his CONFIDENCE *in* the defences.
Never did they COMPLAIN *of* their sufferings.
You should CONGRATULATE him *on* his prowess.
We shall DEPEND *upon* him.
In the morning he was DEPRIVED *of* his farm.
Do you DISAPPROVE *of* my conduct?
The soldiers DISAGREED *with* their officers.
The young men were EAGER *for* war.
One angle is EQUAL *to* another.
Food and water are ESSENTIAL *to* life.
Everyone should be FOND *of* sport.
Our garden is FREE *from* weeds.
Surely you are not IGNORANT *of* the consequences.
The sea-captain was much INDEBTED *to* his men.
Your flowers are INFERIOR *to* mine. .
I LONG *for* the calm of country life.
I do not OBJECT *to* your behaviour.
We must not QUARREL *with* him.
Can we RELY *on* your secrecy?
Your hat is SIMILAR *to* mine.
The pen is not always SUPERIOR *to* the sword.
The knight put his TRUST *in* his white horse.
King John was UNFITTED *for* his high position.

GROUP 2

Is it wise to ABSTAIN *from* eating meat?
We found it possible to ACCEDE *to* his request.
The old man is AFFLICTED *with* rheumatism.
You should AIM *at* gaining a place in the team.
The people BESTOWED great honour *on* Cromwell.
We should COMMUNICATE *with* him *on* the matter.
The people here always COMPLY *with* regulations.
Napoleon was always COVETOUS *of* praise.
The young man was DESERVING *of* reward.
Everyone is DESIROUS *of* winning the prize.
The flood waters ENCROACHED *on* our property.
The inhabitants claimed EXEMPTION *from* tax.

The pauper was GRATEFUL *to* the lady *for* the gift.
I am certain he is GUILTLESS *of* such an act.
The warden INSISTED *on* the adoption of his plan.
A soldier is always JEALOUS *of* his prowess.
Everyone is LIABLE *to* error.
The besieged men had great NEED *of* water.
Many people are POOR *in* worldly goods, but RICH *in* happiness.
The guide PREVAILED *upon* me to accompany him.
She is well QUALIFIED *for* the position.
Do not REFRAIN *from* seeing that picture.
The accused REPENTED *of* his evil acts.
George Washington had a REPUTATION *for* honesty.
We must never RESORT *to* wicked practices.

EXERCISE: Indicate the prepositions to be used after the following:

GROUP 3	GROUP 4	GROUP 5	GROUP 6
annoyed	acquit	abound	accrue
ashamed	aggravated	addicted	alienate
blame	blush	apt	connect
compare	independent	bequeath	connive
disgusted	indulge	dispense	convenient
expert	inspired	emerge	culminate
full	love	impart	discriminate
laugh	partake	impatient	dote
persevere	rejoice	indicative	elicit
prefer	resigned	marred	impervious
respect	strewn	part	inclination
search	subscribe	persist	lavish
slow	substitute	pry	militate
suitable	succumb	recoil	rail
wait	victim	reflect	remonstrate

GROUP 7

Use the following expressions in sentences:

acquiesce *in*
answerable *to*
associated *with*
averse *to*
capacity *for*
derogatory *to*
devoid *of*

dissent *from*
endowed *with*
gloat *over*
inseparable *from*
intent *upon*
necessity *of*
opposite *to*

profit *by*
reconciled *to*
respite *from*
sensitive *to*
sympathize *with*
worthy *of*

GROUP 8

Distinguish between:

angry *at*, angry *with;* confer *on*, confer *with;* consist *of*, consist *in;* disappointed *in*, disappointed *of;* hatred *of*, hatred *for;* hope *of*, hope *for;* offence *at*, offence *against;* responsible *to*, responsible *for;* taste *of*, taste *for;* tired *of*, tired *with;* vexed *with*, vexed *at;* wait *on*, wait *for*.

GROUP 9

Distinguish between:

agree *with*, agree *to;* attend *to*, attend *on;* brought *to*, brought *under;* correspond *to*, correspond *with;* glance *at*, glance *over;* heir *of*, heir *to;* indignant *with*, indignant *at;* influence *over*, influence *on;* invested *with*, invested *in;* smile *at*, smile *on;* sorry *for*, sorry *about;* speak *on*, speak *of*.

PROVERBS

A proverb is a short statement of a truth. From the earliest of times most men have accepted the same conclusion from experience and observation; then one wise man condenses the conclusion into a concise statement which we call a proverb. In the words of one writer:

"A proverb is the wisdom of many and the wit of one."

Sometimes proverbs are written in figurative language. For example, when we say, "Empty vessels make the most sound," we wish to say that people who have the least knowledge and the least merit are apt to be great and foolish talkers and boasters.

Express in your own words the meanings of the following proverbs:

GROUP 1

Look before you leap.
One good turn deserves another.
Two wrongs do not make a right.
All work and no play makes Jack a dull boy.
A stitch in time saves nine.
Take care of the pence and the pounds will take care of themselves.
The early bird catches the worm.
A friend in need is a friend indeed.
Many hands make light work.
A fool and his money are soon parted.

GROUP 2

If the devil finds a man idle, he'll set him to work.
Never put off until tomorrow what can be done today.
A little knowledge is a dangerous thing.
All is not gold that glitters.
The more haste the less speed.
A rolling stone gathers no moss.
Birds of a feather flock together.
A Jack of all trades, a master of none.
Well begun is half done.
A bad workman always blames his tools.

GROUP 3

It is never too late to mend.
Liars have need of good memories.

Those who live in glass houses should not throw stones.
Where there's a will there's a way.
Every cloud has a silver lining.
It is no use crying over spilt milk.
A bird in the hand is worth two in the bush.
A burnt child dreads the fire.
It is a long lane that has no turning.
Wide ears and a short tongue.

GROUP 4

Beauty is only skin deep.
It is too late to close the stable-door when the horse it out.
Do not count your chickens before they are hatched.
One man's meat is another man's poison.
A watched pot never boils.
Between two stools we come to the ground.
An oak is not felled with a single blow.
No pains no gains.
We soon believe what we desire.
When the cat is away the mice will play.

GROUP 5

Strike while the iron is hot.
There is no royal road to learning.
A man may lead a horse to the water, but he cannot make
    it drink.
Don't put all your eggs into one basket.
Constant dripping wears away a stone.
Our worst misfortunes are those that never happen.
Make hay while the sun shines.
Let bygones be bygones.
None so blind as those who will not see.
Rome was not built in a day.

GROUP 6

A drowning man clutches at a straw.
We never know the worth of water till the well is dry.
Misfortune makes strange bedfellows.
He who makes no mistakes makes nothing.
It is easy to be wise after the event.
Every horse thinks his pack the heaviest.
Example is better than precept.
Truth is truth to the end of reckoning.
Speech is silvern, silence golden.
There is no rose without a thorn.

GROUP 7

Do not cross the bridge until you come to it.
Good words without deeds are rushes and reeds.
The cobbler should stick to his last.
The last straw breaks the camel's back.
Fools learn nothing from wise men; but wise men learn
    much from fools.
A straw best shows how the wind blows.
He who excuses himself accuses himself.
Prevention is better than cure.
Money is a good servant but a poor master.
Never spoil the ship for a haporth of tar.

GROUP 8

As you make your bed, so you must lie on it.
Faults are thick where love is thin.
Try your skill in gilt first, and then in gold.
Ill weeds grow apace.
Love lives in cottages as well as in courts.
Busiest men have the most leisure.
He who handles a nettle tenderly is soonest stung.
A saint abroad and a devil at home.
Fools rush in where angels fear to tread.
The mill cannot grind with the water that is past.

GROUP 9

A chain is no stronger than its weakest link.
Too far east is west.
Let sleeping dogs lie.
Rats desert a sinking ship.
It is better to wear out than rust out.
A wise man is never less alone than when alone.
Even the weariest river winds somewhere to the sea.
One should not wash dirty linen in public.
Distant hills are greener.
No physician like a true friend.

GROUP 10

Do not change horses when crossing a stream.
Let not your tongue cut your throat.
Circumstances alter cases.
Experience is the mother of wisdom.
Blood is thicker than water.
One cannot get blood from a stone.

Coming events cast their shadows before.
By their fruits shall you know them.
Desperate diseases need desperate cures.
Still waters run deep.

GROUP 11

Do not look a gift horse in the mouth.
He who touches pitch will be defiled.
What can you expect of a hog but a grunt?
None so deaf as those who will not hear.
Time and tide wait for no man.
Kitchen physic is the best physic.
Admonish your friends in private, praise them in public.
Too much of aught is good for nought.
The leopard cannot change its spots.
Death is the great leveller.

GROUP 12

Cowards die many times before their death.
Fools wander, wise men travel.
What the eye does not see the heart does not grieve.
He who pays the piper can call the tune.
Young men see visions; old men dream dreams.
Necessity is the mother of invention.
Every man is the architect of his own fortune.
History repeats itself.
Time is the great healer.
Mischiefs come by the pound but go away by ounces.

GROUP 13

Lowly sit, richly warm.
You cannot make a silk purse out of a sow's ear.
Where ignorance is bliss 'tis folly to be wise.
When Greek meets Greek, then comes the tug of war.
Catch not at the shadow and lose the substance.
There is a time to wink as well as see.
Sudden friendship, sure repentance.
To err is human, to forgive divine.
No cross, no crown.
It is better to travel hopefully than to arrive.

GROUP 14

Procrastination is the thief of time.
Reckless youth makes rueful age.
The child is father to the man.
A tide taken on the flood leads on to fortune.
Mercy to the criminal may be cruelty to the people.
Many a flower is born to blush unseen.
Beggars cannot be choosers.
Old birds are not caught with the chaff.
Charity begins at home.
Discretion is the better part of valour.

GROUP 15

Happy is the country that has no history.
Liberty is not licence.
The vulgar will keep no account of your hits, but of your
    misses.
Vows made in storms are forgotten in calm.
No man is a hero to his valet.
A crowded hour of glorious life is worth an age without a
    name.
They also serve who only stand and wait.
Sweet are the uses of adversity.
There is a divinity that shapes our ends, rough-hew them
    how we will.
The proper study of mankind is man.

FOREIGN PROVERBS
GROUP 1

Look at his face and don't ask about his circumstances.
    (Persian)
No fly dares approach a boiling pot.   (Spanish)
He who sows thorns should not go barefooted.   (Hindu)
No dispute is possible without an adversary.   (Japanese)
Never try to prove what nobody doubts.   (Arabic)
While it rains fill the jar.   (Turkish)
He who would eat the nut must crack the kernel.   (Latin)
A small leak will sink a great ship.   (German)
All bad flesh smells alike.   (Chinese)
Four horses cannot overtake the tongue.   (Confucius)

GROUP 2

If the first of the wine jar is dregs, what will its last be?
    (Persian)

The best word is the word that remains to be spoken.
    (Spanish)
Sooner or later the strong need the help of the weak.
    (French)
Make peace with men and quarrel with your sins.   (Italian)
Fallen blossoms leave their perfume behind.   (Japanese)
Paradise lies under the feet of mothers.   (The Koran)
The dawn does not come twice to awaken a man.   (Arabic)
Each loss is counsel.   (Turkish)
He who stumbles twice over the same stone is a fool.
    (Latin)
Only rogues feel the restraint of law.   (German)
Where water does not flow it remains at the same level.
    (Chinese)

GROUP 3

The first part of the night think of your own faults; the
    latter, think of the faults of others.   (Chinese)
The sorrows of others are the consolation of fools. (Spanish)
Good doctrine needs no miracle.   (Japanese)
Haste is the sister of repentance.   (Moorish)
No religion without courage.   (Arabic)
Golden words open an iron door.   (Turkish)
Rumour acquires strength in her progress.   (Latin)
Envy eats nothing but its own heart.   (German)
Let him who gives say nothing and him who receives speak
    (Portuguese)
Suspicion makes cables out of spiders' webs.   (German)

BIBLICAL PROVERBS

A soft answer turneth away wrath.
Righteousness exalteth a nation.
The spirit of a man will sustain his infirmity.
Unto the pure all things are pure.
Whatsoever a man soweth, that shall he also reap.
Judge not, that ye be not judged.
If the blind lead the blind, both shall fall into the ditch.
Whosoever will save his life will lose it.
Charity shall cover the multitude of sins.
He that is slow to anger is better than the mighty, and he
    that ruleth his spirit than he that taketh a city.
He that is without sin among us, let him first cast a stone.
A prophet is not without honour except in his own country
    and in his own house.

74

ANTONYMS

Words opposite in meaning are called antonyms.
Write the antonyms of the following words:
N.B. You will notice that some of the words can be used as
different parts of speech. In such cases, you are advised to write
the antonyms for each part of speech.

GROUP 1

new	open	old	first
dirty	love	high	light
rich	hot	sweet	wet
wrong	quick	late	laugh

GROUP 2

sharp	fresh	true	clever
loss	sell	tight	giant
tame	noisy	peaceful	front
rough	cheap	full	lead

GROUP 3

remember	spend	narrow	cruel
whisper	straight	safety	feeble
question	well	nasty	lengthen
arrive	beauty	aloud	raise

GROUP 4

hero	lend	risky	hollow
still	busy	doubtful	shiny
pale	praise	hurry	courage
seize	honour	harsh	vacant

GROUP 5

spectator	sickness	ascend	anger
wholly	slender	future	awkward
youth	scatter	deep	break
together	receive	advance	bloom

GROUP 6

ask	calm	guilt	distant
absence	curse	conceal	employee
destroy	consent	loathe	frequently
omit	conquest	miser	capture

GROUP 7

gradual	faint	freedom	create
generous	fierce	friendly	mansion
famous	dense	neglect	alert
fake	opponent	dawn	anxiety

GROUP 8

departure	aid	chance	cure
allow	always	mercy	pity
attack	heavenly	different	difficult
gather	humorous	misery	amusement

GROUP 9

approach	compliment	haughty	determined
accept	fertile	creditor	keen
command	collect	inferior	rare
curious	prompt	choice	delicious

GROUP 10

delay	decrease	construct	ancient
cause	enough	fickle	foreigner
delicate	excitement	forbid	favour
desperate	flimsy	exterior	folly

GROUP 11

arctic	gratify	quarrelsome	accuse
fascinate	glut	entrance	sultry
gruff	aggression	alarm	excuse
gigantic	permanent	economical	expose

GROUP 12

talkative	admiration	elect	achieve
accidental	provoke	appreciation	earnest
ample	agony	abolish	frivolous
falsify	depression	eager	nervous

GROUP 13

attract	bungle	docile	detach
accede	bankrupt	crude	perfume
spoil	boastful	confuse	discard
enlarge	clear	imaginary	enrage

GROUP 14

acquit	defence	candid	contraction
deny	deposit	despondent	deter
evident	plaintiff	eternal	comparison
damage	relieve	desert	rural

GROUP 15

deceive	adversity	elaborate	impudence
esteem	gravity	serious	expel
diminish	embarrassment	protest	divine
emphasize	expenditure	deficit	harmonious

GROUP 16

ignorant	loneliness	collapse	energetic
important	luxury	niggardly	pester
loyalty	injury	resist	eloquent
maximum	majority	protection	assemble

GROUP 17

ornamental	degraded	reluctant	eminent
evasive	recommend	reckless	superfluous
prologue	hypocrisy	vice	servile
promotion	obstinate	aggravate	exaggerate

GROUP 18

absurd	apologetic	improvement	pollute
vain	acute	extinct	barbarous
voluntary	invaluable	arrogant	observant
vague	affirm	solemn	transparent

GROUP 19

circuitous	defective	blasphemy	ecstasy
celibacy	deformity	majestic	analysis
choleric	spurious	eccentric	nomadic
deciduous	abstruse	exhaustive	reconciliation

GROUP 20

apathetic	affectation	impetuous	procrastinate
indulgent	sterile	noxious	inevitable
industrious	impartial	obsequious	sobriety
penury	imminent	obdurate	vacillation

PHRASES INTO WORDS

Substitute a word for each of the following phrases:

GROUP 1

one who looks after sheep; one in charge of a football match; one who fits and mends pipes for water or gas; one in charge of a railway station; one employed to solve crimes; one employed to put out fires; one employed to keep order in the community; one in charge of a ship; one who shaves beards and cuts hair; one who makes clothes for women; one who makes clothes for men; one who sells goods to the highest bidder; one who drives cattle; one who picks a team to play a game; one who sells fresh vegetables and fruit.

GROUP 2

a place where bread is made; a room or building where books are kept; a room underground for storing goods; a place where fruit is grown; a place for keeping food cool; a platform beside which ships may be loaded; a place where stone is got out of the ground; a place where goods are made; a place where people worship; a place where cars are kept; a place from which a preacher delivers a sermon; a place where clothes are washed; a place where pigs are kept; a place where plays are acted; a place where a dog is housed; a place where a horse is housed.

GROUP 3

to bite a little at a time; a continuous pain; to make a lively sound like a bird; a young lion; the chief city of a state or country; a fight between two persons with weapons; the break of day; unable to speak; unable to hear; the woolly covering of a sheep; not thoroughly dry; a large number of sheep; physically weak; the top of a mountain; to scatter in small drops.

GROUP 4

to look at for a moment; having rough uneven edges and sharp points; the sound of quick light taps or footsteps; without fault; of great value; a gentle sound (as of leaves in a breeze); to throw in all directions; to burn the surface of; a loud sharp cry of pain or fear; to dry up and wrinkle through heat or dryness; a thin stream of liquid; not occupied by anyone; light rain; to breathe out; idle talk about other people.

GROUP 5

sweet-scented; to give a weak unsteady light; without any doubt; punishment meted out by a judge; a great number of fish; to boil gently; to burn slowly without flame; to walk wearily; to disappear suddenly; to walk lamely; food made from grain; ungraceful in movement; a poor, dirty home; a rising of sailors, etc., against their officers; to beat violently with a whip or rope.

GROUP 6

a large spoon with a long handle; a low, continuous, indistinct sound; the son of one's brother or sister; a plane figure with eight sides and eight angles; the roof of the mouth; a new member of a society, group, etc.; the bony framework of an animal body; a tall, slender pointed structure on a building; to start growing; not false; taking place by degrees; a person who competes with another; firmly fixed; to tread under foot; one who ill-uses weaker persons.

GROUP 7

very bright; a mischievous trick; to cut into two equal parts; to make unable to see clearly because of too much light; to go down; to give great pleasure to; to say no to a person; to be silent because of bad temper; to seize firmly; each day; not easy; one who pays rent for the use of property; a pile of hay in the open air; very sharp and high-pitched in sound, of very fine character.

GROUP 8

a school for very young children; a child whose father and mother are dead; separate divisions of glass in a window; alike in every respect; a person under the care of a doctor; a very fast train; to walk in a leisurely manner; to give oneself up to the enemy; without delay; to send out flashes of light; anxious and eager to find out; the outer parts of a city; the arms and legs of a person, to put right; a person entertained at another's house.

GROUP 9

to set free; free from pride; to fall in or down suddenly; to run into or come together violently; to say one is not satisfied; highly delightful to the taste; to fail in obtaining what was hoped for or expected; easily heard or seen; very great; having, or showing, little or no knowledge; to stand about; a sudden roll to one side; to treat too kindly; to quarrel about an unimportant matter; a great rush of water.

GROUP 10

sweet-sounding; to deepen water by bringing up mud; great fear; an unmarried man; an unmarried woman; easily frightened; desire for food; a number of people gathered in a church for worship; the mouth of a volcano; a room for hospital patients; people saved from a shipwreck; a man who goes to another country to teach religion; a closed fireplace for melting metals; a place where dead people are buried; to make less.

GROUP 11

a wound caused by hot steam or liquid; not plentiful; to make land ready for seed; badly and poorly dressed; to hang or swing loosely; an angry look; of poor quality; to drink in small amounts; a written acknowledgement of money or goods received; to repeat aloud from memory; to feel about uncertainly with the hands; a scheme to trick people out of money; in uniform order or at fixed intervals; causing death; to arrange and to put in working order.

GROUP 12

a place where a wild animal lives; a place where a king or an archbishop lives; a place where monks live; a place where grain is stored; a place where aeroplanes are kept; a place where birds are kept; a place where fish are kept; a place where bees are kept; a building where goods are stored; a platform on a ship where the captain and his officers stand; a building where objects of natural history, etc., are stored; a place where physical exercises are practised; a place where money is coined; a place where young plants are raised for transplanting; a place where water is stored.

GROUP 13

a passage between rows of seats, especially in a church; the faint light before sunrise or after sunset; to conceal oneself by altering one's appearance; a narrow passage between two buildings; one who is learning a trade; rude or lacking in manners; the mixture of gases surrounding the earth; a loud cry of anger or pain; faithfulness to duty or to friends; the mouth of a river up which the tide runs; a bride's clothes or outfit; to bring goods into a country; to send goods out of a country; a person sent away from his country as a punishment; a song for two people.

GROUP 14

a wall of stones built to stop waves; done on purpose; easily harmed; to break into small pieces; the ability to do something well; a long distance race on foot; of or near the South Pole; what is usual or average; a favourable time or chance; covered with dark clouds; a story designed to teach a moral lesson; a rather steep face of a cliff; to walk with no special aim; likely to happen; a set of four.

GROUP 15

firmness of purpose; a conversation between two people; a wide area; the people born about the same time; an old story handed down from the past (usually of a marvellous nature); separation from others until there is no danger of spreading disease; no longer in existence; to free a prisoner upon payment; too hasty; a typist who can use shorthand; to kill by stopping the breathing; to put out (a fire, etc.); a ruler with absolute power; a small open boat; to go faster and faster.

GROUP 16

loss of respect or honour; a strong dislike; a sudden and violent twist or pull; to cause air to move in and out freely; the giving back of injury for injury; to break the quiet or order of; the claw of a bird of prey; a feeling of pity or tenderness for; to give the meaning in another language; to give out something among people or in different places; to walk or behave in a self-important manner; bad tempered and unfriendly; savagely cruel; very bright or very clear; to make someone feel sure.

GROUP 17

the time of the year when day and night are equal; a journey made for some definite purpose; ploughed but not sown; to explain using pictures, etc.; living forever; a neck of land connecting two larger bodies of land; easily understood or seen; past the time fixed (for arrival, etc.); easily bent; standing out; to make known to the public; to become ill again after getting well; easily hurt (feelings), not pretending; a feeling that something is wrong.

GROUP 18

one who designs buildings, etc.; one who studies the stars; one who studies plants; one who makes women's hats; one employed by a dressmaker to wear and show off clothes; one who makes or sells instruments for the eyesight; one who conducts people to their seats in a theatre; one in charge of an orchestra; one who puts glass in windows; one who carves figures; one who works in stone; one skilled in foreign languages; one who sells writing material; one who uses instruments for healing; one who answers a telephone at a telephone exchange.

GROUP 19

one who manages the business affairs of another; an agreement to stop fighting for a time; a mass of snow, stones, etc., falling from a mountain; to mark an event by some form of entertainment; one who gathers news for a newspaper; to express to a person pleasure at his good fortune; to take off (e.g., an amount from an account); able to do things well; the leaves on trees; to escape from; lower in quality, etc.; having (showing) a not too high opinion of oneself; something that prevents progress or makes a thing difficult; to bear the weight of; a noticeable difference when set side by side.

GROUP 20

to look at with pleasure and respect; a list of months and days in the year; to tell one's faults or sins; to allow to enter; showing thanks for a favour received; a carriage for carrying a coffin; a sudden bursting with a loud noise; an uninhabited or waste place; able to be seen; to go on board a ship; an opinion given about what to do; very foolish; an exciting or dangerous event; a written direction for medicine from a doctor to a chemist, the colour of one's skin.

GROUP 21

For each of the following expressions the word substituted must be a verb ending in "—fy".

to make into a liquid; to make pleasing to look at; to calm and quieten; to dull the senses; to prove to be the same; to cause pleasure; to fill with great fear; to put right; to make known; to prove or show to be right and just; to make incorrect or untrue; to give evidence; to show by example; to make up for damage done; to speak ill of.

GROUP 22

the science of farming; something that acts against poison; a regular payment made to a person no longer at work; applicable to the matter in hand; slightly open (of doors); close and warm; a name by which a person hides his real name; to get down or off (bus, etc.); to put off to a future date; earliest known inhabitants; to work flour into dough; a room, etc., provided for a visitor; to give false evidence in a court of justice; to speak fast with very little sense; lasting from year to year.

GROUP 23

to drive a tenant out of a house; to gather together; a false statement against a person's reputation; a published statement damaging a person's reputation; a room within the roof of a house; a person who owes money; an arranged list of articles; of the usual or ordinary standard; the one hundredth anniversary; one who gives his life for a good cause; a five-sided figure; to comfort one in sorrow; an eating into or a wearing away; in a secret manner; fit for human beings to live in.

GROUP 24

a decision of a jury; to make more beautiful or gay; to explain the meaning of (e.g., a word); light blue; to refuse to obey or show respect; to feel contempt for; a story of a man's life, written by himself; to prevent from leaving; standing clearly in view; to inject some liquid under the skin to prevent disease; unable to be captured by force of arms; something left to a person by will; to work or act together; to exchange opinions on a subject; to make secret plans (especially to do wrong).

GROUP 25

not easily annoyed; a sudden and strong attack; a flaw which spoils the appearance, etc.; to sail round; one sent by others to act or speak for them; a person pretending to be what he is not; to state that one is against; to mock and laugh at; the land through which a river flows by many outlets to the sea; the use of remarks aimed at hurting the feelings; one who is new in any business, etc.; deliberate damage to equipment, etc.; a space completely empty, even of air; to rub out; to eat greedily or to swallow up.

GROUP 26

an undertaking in which there is risk; to change the nature of; the plant life of a place or country; the animal life of a place or country; a word having a similar meaning to another; to turn a thing away from a straight path; above all others; to come or go before; a benefit enjoyed by one or a few only; to strengthen by adding more material; of different kinds; acting only after careful thought; to rule unjustly or harshly; always ready to attack; to desire very much (another's property).

GROUP 27

to prevent free movement; to put out of the usual shape; goods bought and sold; fighting spirit; difficult to persuade; to watch carefully; a great number (especially people); great need; a form of writing meant to make something appear foolish; odd or peculiar (in conduct); to tempt away; a long existing quarrel; to feel sorry for having done wrong; a planet moving around another; to discuss in order to reach an agreement.

GROUP 28

the regular way of doing things; to come to an end; to put up with; to pull down or to pieces; to send back a foreigner to his own country; to do well; wearisome or monotonous; natural power to do something; to say that something must not be done; done or said with authority; the power of doing or saying the right thing at the right moment; the art of moving forces when in battle; the breaking of a law; to lay waste; (of animals) not wild.

GROUP 29

For each of the following expressions the word substituted must end in "—ent".

a piece broken off; a state of being satisfied; to think out something new (a machine, etc.); working with care and not wasting time; that can be seen; an arrangement to meet someone; a suite of rooms forming a complete dwelling; not worrying or caring about somebody or something; an expression of praise; to become less severe or harsh; a putting off to another time; of a kind nature; ready to happen; having power over all; not relying on anyone else.

GROUP 30

causing a feeling of fear or mystery; a person who is one hundred years old; one who acts or speaks in imitation of another; to put or keep away from others; to defeat by cunning; a general principle put forward as an explanation; not given to much speaking; to go on doing something even against difficulties; strong in growth; easy to understand; to level to the ground; to get well after an illness; future generations; to feel or express great sorrow; having a sour smell or taste.

GROUP 31

given to silly conduct; causing great misfortune; happening as if of its own accord; orderly behaviour; easily bent or influenced; a period of ten years; out of date; anything on a small or reduced scale; within easy reach; to reduce the strength of a liquid by adding water; one who held a position before another; belonging to the earliest ages of man; likely to last for a long time; to make laws; a statement that appears contradictory but is true.

GROUP 32

a mixture of two or more metals; equal in value; to cause uneasiness to; not respectable; inability to sleep; a desire to do harm to somebody; the treating with disrespect of something sacred; known facts (from which to draw conclusions); lacking something; to trick a person out of what is rightly his; more than is necessary; by surprise; the saving of property from loss by a disaster (especially at sea); a great show; fully grown.

GROUP 33

For each of the following expressions the word substituted must be a verb ending in "—ate".

to hold by a spell; to put up with; to give all one's attention to something; to lower in one's own opinion or in that of others; to pass oneself off as; to perform some duty; to make new again; to destroy all; to make a way into or through; to enquire into; to calm one who has been offended; to put forward a person's name so that he may be chosen for a position; to take part in; to restore to consciousness; to influence by frightening.

GROUP 34

depressed in spirits; of mixed kinds; of, or happening in the night; a heavy downpour of water; an animal able to live on land and in water; without things necessary for life (e.g., food and clothes); a district under the care of a bishop; one who wanders with no fixed home; not clearly seen or understood; knowing everything; a wide uninterrupted view; not allowing light to pass through; anything (particularly a liquid) which gives one a temporary increase of power; one who uses his money for the good of his fellow men; bitter regret for wrong done.

GROUP 35

word for word; an exact copy; having considerable powers of invention; with want of proper care; passed on from one generation to another; holding firmly (property, rights, etc.); extremely hungry; to talk to oneself; worthy of respect because of age, character, etc.; a fault-finding person who can see nothing good in human nature; that cannot make mistakes; of far too great a price; without preparation; on the surface only; using more words than are wanted.

IDIOMS

Idioms are expressions which often have meanings other than their logical or grammatical ones. However, they have been in our language for so long a time, and their meanings are so clear to us that we accept them. One writer aptly wrote of them: "In their brevity, vigour and unusualness, they are the life and spirit of language."

Explain the following idiomatic expressions:

GROUP 1

with open arms; a black sheep; sour grapes; the lion's share; a needle in a haystack; to play the game; to burn one's fingers; in hot water; to be in the same boat; a bird's eye view; a drop in the bucket; to keep the ball rolling; once in a blue moon; a clean sweep; to nip in the bud.

GROUP 2

as the crow flies; with half an eye; to cry for the moon; in one's good (bad) books; to make one's mouth water; the man in the street; to miss the bus; to paddle one's own canoe; a turn-coat; the pot calling the kettle black; to pull one's weight; to have seen better days; to sink or swim; for a song; to take pot luck.

GROUP 3

a wild goose-chase; to talk shop; to throw a spanner in the works; a right-hand man; by leaps and bounds; to have one's heart in one's mouth; to rub shoulders; to coin money; to ride for a fall; a white lie; to keep a straight face; to have a long face; to be two-faced: to the death; to eat one's cake and have it too.

GROUP 4

to make one's hair stand on end; to be under a cloud; out of one's depth; to show one's hand; to wash one's hands; to keep (lose) one's head; to keep one's head above water; to step off on the wrong foot; to bite the dust; on the carpet; a dog in the manger; to bury the hatchet; to look daggers; thin (thick)-skinned; against the grain.

GROUP 5

a feather in one's cap; to feather one's nest; cap in hand; to have all one's eggs in one basket; down at heels; to kill the goose that laid the golden eggs; to leave no stone unturned; an ugly duckling; to have one's hands full; to play a double game; to kill two birds with the one stone; to make a mountain out of a molehill; when my ship comes in; to hold out the olive branch; a shot in the dark.

GROUP 6

to skate on thin ice; a sleeping partner; a stab in the back; to keep someone in the dark; a fish out of water; to drive into a corner; to play with fire; a snake in the grass; to get into a rut; to keep the wolf from the door; to cry wolf; to turn a person's head; to put down one's foot; to cool one's heels; to have no backbone.

GROUP 7

to slip through one's fingers; to swallow the bait; to be at the top of the ladder; a fairweather friend; afraid of his own shadow; to rest on one's oars; open-handed; a friend at court; with flying colours; to throw off the mask; to catch at a straw; the last straw; to strike oil; to be at daggers drawn; to fall between two stools.

GROUP 8

a bird of passage; to have a second string to one's bow; to beard the lion in his den; with one's back to the wall; winning one's spurs; to tread on slippery ground; on the rocks; a square peg in a round hole; to enter the lists; to weather the storm; tooth and nail; a fool's paradise; to keep at arm's length; to carry coals to Newcastle; an open sesame.

GROUP 9

an armchair critic; to ask for bread and receive a stone; a clean slate; to open one's eyes; to gird up one's loins; with gloves off; to hold one's hand; with clean hands; to burn the candle at both ends; to take (lose) heart; to play to the gallery; a rough diamond; to draw the line; to fall upon one's feet; to build upon sand.

GROUP 10

a burning question; a fellow traveller; with one foot in the grave; to hand on the torch; a pot-boiler; to grasp the nettle; to lose caste; to stand in another person's shoes; to throw down (pick up) the gauntlet; to run the gauntlet; with a jaundiced eye; to go with the stream; to split hairs; to die in harness; an itching palm.

GROUP 11

a good Samaritan; the handwriting on the wall; a prodigal son; a Job's comforter; a doubting Thomas; to kill the fatted calf; to cut the Gordian Knot; the sword of Damocles; Achilles' heel; an Herculean task; a Parthian shaft; to cross the Rubicon; a Pyrrhic victory, between Scylla and Charybdis; a Frankenstein.

GROUP 12

to stir up a hornet's nest; a storm in a teacup; to put one's hand to the plough; born in the purple; a red-letter day; to rob Peter to pay Paul; a rope of sand; a bed of roses; the salt of the earth; to turn over a new leaf; to run with the hare and hunt with the hounds; out of the wood; to see the light; to hide one's light under a bushel; in a bee line.

GROUP 13

to fish in troubled waters; a leap in the dark; to have too many irons in the fire; to be in the clouds; a cross to bear; to cry from the housetops; an oily tongue; to go through fire and water; to make ends meet; a broken reed; to read between the lines; to have an axe to grind; a bull in a china shop; to burn one's boats; feet of clay.

GROUP 14

crocodile tears; on the rack; to play with edged tools; a bolt from the blue; to pour oil on troubled waters; to worship the golden calf; to bring grist to the mill; the sear and yellow leaf; in sackcloth and ashes; to claim one's pound of flesh; to cast pearls before swine; to bear (give) the palm; a left-handed compliment; to hoist with one's own petard; a stormy petrel.

TWENTY PRONUNCIATION GROUPS
GROUP 1

ADDRESS ....Accent the second syllable.

ADVERTISE ....Accent the first syllable.

ADVERTISEMENT ....Accent the second syllable.

BECAUSE ....The second syllable may be pronounced *-koz* or *-kawz*.

BOW ....(a) For arrows, for playing the violin, and thirdly, the knot — rhymes with LOW.

(b) Of a ship, to submit, and to bend the body — rhymes with COW.

DIAMOND ....This word has three syllables.

ENGINE ....The first syllable is pronounced *en-*, not *in*.

LIBRARY ....This word has three syllables. Do not say *libery*.

PERHAPS ....Sound the H. Do not say *praps* or *per-raps'*.

SWALLOW ....*Swol'lo*. The last syllable rhymes with GO. Avoid pronouncing the second syllable *-ler*. Now say:

YELLOW	SHALLOW
FELLOW	HOLLOW
FOLLOW	BURROW

GROUP 2

ATE ....Rhymes with SET or PLATE. The former is preferable

BURGLAR ....Two syllables. The error commonly made is to insert a second U in the word.

CEMETERY ....Three syllables.

FAULT ....*fawlt*.

FEMININE ....The last syllable rhymes with FIN; not with FINE.

FIGURE ....Rhymes with TRIGGER.

ITALIAN ....The first syllable is pronounced *it-*; not *eye-*.

MONASTERY ....Three syllables.

QUARTER	*kwor'ter.* Make sure you pronounce both R's.
SAYS	*sez.*
SOFTEN	The T is silent. It is also silent in FASTEN HASTEN MOISTEN GLISTEN LISTEN OFTEN

GROUP 3

AGAIN	Rhymes with either MEN or MAIN.
APOSTLE	The T is silent. It is also silent in BUSTLE NESTLE TRESTLE EPISTLE RUSTLE WHISTLE JOSTLE THISTLE
DIFFERENCE	Three syllables.
ENGLAND	*Ing'gland;* also ENGLISH, pronounced *Ing'glish.*
FEBRUARY	Four syllables — accent the first. Make sure the second syllable is pronounced *-rew.*
GEOGRAPHY	Four syllables.
GEOMETRY	Four syllables.
GHOST	The H is silent. It is silent in the following GH words: GHETTO GHASTLY GHOUL GHERKIN
QUAY	*key.*
SURPRISE	Make sure that you do not say *sup-.*

GROUP 4

BRITAIN	*Brit'n.*
CLERK	*klark.*
HALT	*hawlt.*
HOTEL HUMOUR	} The H is sounded.

Here is a list of some of the words in which the H is sounded. Practise them.

HONEY	HUMID
HOME	HUNGER
HOLE	HURRICANE
HOBBLE	HUMAN
HOLLY	HURDLE
HORIZON	HUE
HOPE	HOWEVER
HORDE	HUNDRED
HUMBLE	HURRY

MAYOR .... Rhymes with GLARE.

SIMILAR .... Three syllables.

WHICH .... ⎫
WHIP .... ⎬ The *HW* sound is preferred to the
WHISTLE .... ⎭ *W* sound so as to preserve a useful
sound group. Also in:

WHEN	WHILE
WHENCE	WHIMPER
WHERE	WHIRL
WHETHER	WHEEL
WHEY	WHEAT
WHIG	WHITHER

GROUP 5

ACQUIRE .... *ak-kwire'*.

ADULTS .... The Oxford Dictionary accents the second syllable; B.B.C., the first.

ATHLETE .... *ath'leet*. There are two syllables.

CHAOS .... *kay'oss*.

CONTRIBUTE .... Accent the second syllable.

CORPS .... *kor*. The plural, which is CORPS, is pronounced *korz*. Note that CORPSE is pronounced *korps*.

COURTEOUS .... ⎫ Pronounce the first syllable *kert'-*.
COURTESY .... ⎬ Consult your dictionary for the
difference in meaning and pronunciation between COURTESY and CURTSY.

SUPPRESS .... The first syllable is *sup-*; careless people say *sir-*.

WIZARD   . ...The -ARD is pronounced like -ED
in WICKED. The same sound is in:

MUSTARD	DRUNKARD
STEWARD	COWARD
LEOPARD	BLIZZARD
STANDARD	LIZARD

GROUP 6

ALLY
ALLIES   .} Accent the second syllable.
ALLIED
COMRADE   The first syllable rhymes with TOM.
DISHONEST   The H is not sounded. Practise the
                  following words, in which the H is
                  silent.

HEIR	HONOURABLE
HEIRESS	HONORARY
HONEST	HOSTLER
HONESTY	HOUR
HONOUR	

ENVELOPE   . The first syllable is *en-*, not *on-*.
FRONTIER   The first syllable rhymes with
                  HUNT.
LIGHTNING   . There are two syllables. Do not
                  confuse the word with LIGHTEN-
                  ING.
SALT   *sawlt* or *solt.*
SUPERB   *soo-perb'.* The first syllable rhymes
                  with TOO.

GROUP 7

ABDOMEN   . Accent the first syllable. Also
                  permissible is the accent on the
                  second syllable, -DO-, rhyming with
                  SO.
ADMIRABLE .   .....Accent the first syllable.

ARCTIC ....*ark'tik*. Note also ANTARCTIC.

BISCUIT ....The U is silent. It is also silent in each of the following words. Say them.

CIRCUIT	LIQUOR
CONDUIT	GUILT
GUARANTEE	MASQUERADE
GUILLOTINE	MOSQUITO
GUERILLA	ROGUISH
GUITAR	GUISE

BRILLIANT ....*bril'yent*.

IODINE ....The last syllable rhymes with MINE.

MEDICINE ....*med'sn*.

MISCHIEVOUS ....Accent the first syllable.

ROUTE ....*root*. Do not confuse with the word R O U T, which rhymes with SHOUT.

POMEGRANATE ....*pom'-*. The first E is silent.

GROUP 8

ALMS ....*ahmz*. The L is silent. It is also silent in:

ALMOND	QUALM	CAULK
BALM	STALK	BAULK

COMMUNIST ....Accent the first syllable.

CONSTABLE ....(a) Policeman — First syllable rhymes with SUN.
(b) Family name—First syllable rhymes with DON.

DATA ....*day'ta*.

FASCISM ....⎫
FASCIST ....⎭ Pronounce SC as S.

GENUINE ....The last syllable rhymes with FIN; not with FINE.

PREMIER ....*prem'-*; not *preem'-*.

TATTOO ....Accent the second syllable for both noun and verb.

WRENCH ....The W is silent. It is also silent in the following words. Practise them.

WRAP	WRIGGLE
WREN	WRIST
WRECK	WRONG
WRETCHED	WRATH
WRING	WRY
WRINKLE	WREATH

GROUP 9

BADE — *bad.*

CELTIC . — Pronounce the first C as S; not as K.

COTTAGE — The -AGE is pronounced as *-ij.* The same sound is in the following:

FORAGE	DAMAGE
FUSELAGE	MANAGE
GARBAGE	CARNAGE
COURAGE	ESPIONAGE
VILLAGE	HOSTAGE
SAVAGE	TONNAGE

FORECASTLE — *fok'sl.* The O is long, as in GO.

ISSUE — *.ish'ew.*

MISSILE — .Accent the first syllable; the second rhymes with MILE.

MUNICIPAL — Accent -NIC-, which is pronounced *nis.* It is incorrect to accent the first syllable.

PATHOS — *..pay'thoss.*

PATRON } The pronunciation *pay'-* for the
PATRIOT } first syllable is preferable to *pat'-.*

GROUP 10

AMATEUR — Accent the first syllable. The last syllable rhymes with MURE. The B.B.C. prefers it to rhyme with FUR.

CHAUFFEUR — *sho'fer.* The first syllable rhymes with GO.

CONTRARY ....Accent the first syllable. When the meaning is SELF-WILLED, accent the second, and pronounce the last two syllables to rhyme with FAIRY.

FORMIDABLE ....Accent the first syllable.

GRATIS ....*gray'tis.*

INDOLENT ....Accent the first syllable.

MARTIAL ....*mah'shl.* Note also that PARTIAL is pronounced *pah'shl.*

SCEPTRE ....The C is silent. It is also silent in the following words:

SCIMITAR   SCENE
SCISSORS   SCENT
ABSCESS

SKI ....*she* or *ske.*

SOVIET ....*so'vee-et.* Pronounce the O as in GO.

GROUP 11

ABSENT ....(a) Adjective — accent the first syllable.
(b) Verb — accent the second syllable. The same applies to FREQUENT   PERFECT

ACCOMPLISH ....*-kom'-* is preferable to *-kum'-.*

ARTISAN ....Accent the last syllable, which is pronounced *-zan.*

CATALOGUE ....The last syllable is pronounced *-log.* Now say:

DIALOGUE   MONOLOGUE
EPILOGUE   PROLOGUE

FALCON ....*faw'ken.*

GONDOLA ....Accent the first syllable.

HOSPITABLE ....Accent the first syllable.

ORCHID ....*or'kid.*

PORCELAIN ....*por'slin.* The second syllable rhymes with THIN.

RESPITE ....*res'pit.* The second syllable rhymes with FIT

GROUP 12

Examine the following sets of words of similar spelling. What conclusion did you reach?

AC'CENT (n.)	AC-CENT' (v.)
CON'DUCT (n.)	CON-DUCT' (v.)
CON'FLICT (n.)	CON-FLICT' (v.)
CON'TRACT (n.)	CON-TRACT' (v.)
CON'TEST (n.)	CON-TEST' (v.)
CON'VERT (n.)	CON-VERT' (v.)
CON'VICT (n.)	CON-VICT' (v.)
CON'VOY (n.)	CON-VOY' (v.)
DE'CREASE (n.)	DE-CREASE' (v.)
DE'TAIL (n.)	DE-TAIL' (v.)
DIS'COUNT (n.)	DIS-COUNT' (v.)
ES'CORT (n.)	ES-CORT' (v.)

Consult your dictionary for the following trisyllables. Each can be used as a noun or verb. Note carefully any change in accent.

ATTRIBUTE	OVERCHARGE
INTERCHANGE	RECOMPENSE
MISCONDUCT	REPRIMAND

GROUP 13

Here is another group of disyllables of similar spelling, but different accentuation.

EX'PORT (n.)	EX-PORT' (v.)
EX'TRACT (n.)	EX-TRACT' (v.)
IM'PORT (n.)	IM-PORT' (v.)
IN'CREASE (n.)	IN-CREASE' (v.)
IN'SULT (n.)	IN-SULT' (v.)
OB'JECT (n.)	OB-JECT' (v.)
SUR'VEY (n.)	SUR-VEY' (v.)
SUS'PECT (n.)	SUS-PECT' (v.)
TRANS'PORT (n.)	TRANS-PORT' (v.)
TRANS'FER (n.)	TRANS-FER' (v.)

See what you can discover from your dictionary about the pronunciation and accentuation of the following. Each can be used as a noun or verb.

DESERT	PROGRESS	RECORD
PRESENT	PROJECT	REFUSE
PRODUCE	REBEL	

GROUP 14

CAPITALIST ....Accent the first syllable.

AERIAL ....Pronounce the first syllable as *air-* for both noun and adjective.

FETE ....*fate.* Rhymes with MATE.

GALA ....*gah'la.*

GESTURE ....The G is soft, and is sounded like J. Practise the following words which are similarly pronounced.

GELATINE	GIBE
GELIGNITE	GIBLET
GENDER	GENTILE
GENERATE	GENTRY
GENESIS	GENITIVE
GESTICULATE	GENIUS

LABORATORY ....Accent the first or second syllable.

LUSCIOUS ....*lush'us.*

REPUTABLE ....Accent the first syllable, which is pronounced *rep'-.*

ROMANCE ....Accent the first syllable for the noun, the second for the verb.

TRAIT ....*tray.* The B.B.C. prefers *trayt,* rhyming with WAIT.

GROUP 15

ASPIRANT ....Accent the first syllable: *ass'-,* or accent the second syllable and pronounce it *-spire'-.*

ATTORNEY ....The second syllable is accentuated, and rhymes with HER.

COMPARABLE ....Accent the first syllable.

CONTRALTO ....The second syllable rhymes with SHALL.

ECONOMICS	The first syllable is pronounced *ee-*; not *ek-*.
FRAGILE	*fraj'ile.* The second syllable rhymes with MILE. The pronunciation *fraj'ill* is frequently heard and has dictionary authority. Note that the G is soft, and is sounded like J. Practise the following words which are also pronounced with a soft G.

LONGITUDE   ORGY
LONGEVITY   PAGEANT
LEGITIMATE

KORAN	*kor'an.* The second syllable rhymes with FAN.
MIGRATORY	The first syllable is accented and pronounced *my-*.
PERSONNEL	Accent the last syllable.
TRAVERSE	Accent the first syllable for the noun, and the second for the verb.

GROUP 16

CHASM	CH is pronounced K.
COMMANDANT	The accent is on the last syllable. Note that in COMMANDER the accent is on the second syllable
CONSIGN	The G is silent. Say the following words, which also have a silent G: CONDIGN FEIGN MALIGN DEIGN ARRAIGN IMPUGN
ILLUSTRATIVE	The accent is on the second syllable. Note, however, that ILLUSTRATE is accented on the first syllable.
INTESTINAL	Accent on the second syllable. The B.B.C. prefers it on the third.
INVENTORY	Accent the first syllable.

NAPHTHA ....*naf'tha*. The first syllable of NAPHTHALENE is likewise pronounced *naf'-*.

PSALM ....*sahm*. The P is silent; similarly,

PSEUDONYM   PSYCHIATRY
PSALTER   PNEUMONIA
PSYCHOLOGY   PNEUMATIC

SPA ....*spah.*

THRALL ....*thrawl.*

GROUP 17

ACETIC ....*as-seet'-tik*. The second syllable rhymes with MEET.

ASCETIC ....*as-set'-ik*. The second syllable rhymes with WET.

DETERIORATE ....This word has five syllables. The error commonly made is to omit the fourth.

EXQUISITE ....*eks'kwiz-it*. Accent the first syllable.

FRAGRANT ....*fray'grent;* not *frag'grent*. The long A is likewise found in:

FLAGRANT   VAGRANT

HYPOCRISY ....The first syllable is HYP-; not HY-.

INFAMOUS ....*in'fa-mus.*

RESEARCH ....Accent the second syllable.

RHEUMATISM ....The H is silent. It is also silent in the following words. Practise them.

RHAPSODY   RHUBARB
RHETORIC   RHYME
RHEUM   RHYTHM
RHINOCEROS   RHYTHMIC
RHOMBUS

STATUS ....*stay'tus.*

GROUP 18

ACUMEN .... *ak-kew'men*.

CLANDESTINE ....*klan-des'tin*. It is incorrect to place the accent on the first syllable.

CONVERSANT ... ... Accent the first syllable. It is wrong to accent the second.

DIPHTHONG .... Pronounce the first syllable as *dif*. The pronunciation *dip'thong* is supported by some authorities. DIPHTHERIA is a word in the same class.

EVOLUTION . ...*ee-* or *ev-*.

EXTEMPORE .... This word has four syllables.

IRREPARABLE ....Accent the second syllable. Do the same for IRREFUTABLE.

MEDIOCRE ....The first syllable is pronounced *me'-* not *med'-*.

OBDURATE .... Accent the first syllable.

POSTHUMOUS ....The H is silent. Accent the first syllable and pronounce it to rhyme with LOST.

GROUP 19

CENTRIFUGAL .. .... Accent the second syllable *-trif-*. The accent on the third syllable is wrong.

CLIQUE .... *kleek;* not *klick*.

COGNIZANT .... Accent the first syllable: *kog*.

FLACCID .... *flak'sid*.

MACHINATION ... ... Pronounce the CH as K.

PHARMACEUTICAL . The third syllable is pronounced *-sew-*, to rhyme with FEW. The Oxford Dictionary allows *-kew-* as a variant.

PRIVACY .... *pry'-* or *priv'-*.

SLOUGH ....(a) A swamp — rhymes with PLOUGH.
(b) Snake's skin — rhymes with ENOUGH.

SONOROUS ....Accent the second syllable.

SOUGH ....Rhymes with PLOUGH or rhymes with ENOUGH.

GROUP 20

ACOUSTIC ....*ak-kous'tik* or *ak-koos'tik.*

CONJUGAL ....Accent the first syllable — *kon'-.*

CULINARY ....*kew'-.*

DISPUTANT ....Accent the first syllable.

HEINOUS ....*hay'nus.*

OMNISCIENT ....Accent the second syllable and pronounce it *-nis'-.* The Oxford Dictionary prefers *-nish'-.*

PREMATURE ....*prem'-* is preferable to *pree'-.*

RECONNAISSANCE ..Accent the second syllable *-kon'-.*

REPLICA ....Accent the first syllable, *rep'-.*

VEHEMENT ....There are three syllables, and the H is not sounded.

PRONUNCIATION EXERCISES

Consult your dictionary for the following words. Indicate the error which is made sometimes in the pronunciation of each.

GROUP 1	GROUP 2	GROUP 3	GROUP 4
anything	chestnut	descent	almanac
Australia	cruel	describe	anoint
chocolate	elect	forehead	chimney
fiend	heroine	halfpenny	gigantic
giant	history	lieutenant	interesting
policeman	horrible	ordinarily	Saturday
probably	million	postman	tragedy
speaking	naturally	produce	Tuesday
usually	regular	relieve	twelfth
wreaths	running	umbrella	waistcoat

GROUP 5	GROUP 6	GROUP 7	GROUP 8
dance	debris	admiralty	billiards
electricity	despicable	asphalt	casualty
paragraph	familiar	divest	chivalrous
pasture	government	elastic	finance
pianist	greasy	extraordinary	frigid
postpone	malt	persuade	intellectual
secretary	resistance	quinine	prejudice
shepherd	temporarily	routine	righteous
superintendent	valet	suit	simultaneous
toward	voluntary	suite	superfluous

GROUP 9	GROUP 10	GROUP 11	GROUP 12
aristocrat	aquatic	adept	annihilate
decade	centenary	armistice	annuity
decadent	commentary	buoyant	deficit
gallant	contemplative	cenotaph	epitome
gill	disciplinary	erroneous	gratuity
initial	equilibrium	mauve	harangue
panorama	harass	nomenclature	incalculable
temperance	nuptial	obsequious	irascible
tepid	sapphire	succinct	satiety
tyrannical	silhouette	viands	tuberculosis

"OUGH" WORDS

Here is an interesting test with twelve words ending in OUGH. How would you pronounce them?

borough	dough	rough	though
bough	furlough	slough	through
cough	plough	sough	trough

CORRECTION OF FAULTY SENTENCES

NOUNS

(Rules 1 — 6)

1. When the simple subject consists of one singular noun (or noun equivalent), a singular verb is required.

A knowledge of such matters give men confidence . . . . . .
INCORRECT.
A knowledge of such matters gives men confidence . . . . . .
CORRECT.

The simple subject "knowledge" is singular; therefore, the verb must be singular—"gives."

2. When the subject consists of two or more singular nouns (or noun equivalents) joined by "and", a plural verb is usually required.

Tom and Jack is in the library . . . INCORRECT.
Tom and Jack are in the library . . . CORRECT.

However, when the nouns of the subject are so closely related in thought that they may be considered as a unit, a singular verb is used.

A block and tackle was used . . . CORRECT.

3. When two singular nouns of the subject refer to the same person or thing, the verb must be singular.

Look carefully at these sentences. Can you explain why both are correct? How do they differ in meaning?

A thief and murderer has escaped from prison.
A thief and a murderer have escaped from prison.

4. Do not use a noun and its pronoun as nominatives to the same verb.

The criminal he has escaped . . . INCORRECT.
The criminal has escaped . . . CORRECT.

5. When the subject consists of two nouns (or noun equivalents) joined by "as well as", "and not", or "with", the verb should agree with the noun (or noun equivalent) preceding "as well as", etc.

The great musician, as well as his two sons, were present . . .
INCORRECT.
The great musician, as well as his two sons, was present . . .
CORRECT.

We use the singular verb "was", because we wish to emphasize "great musician". If, however, we wish to give equal emphasis to "great musician" and "his two sons", we should use "and" instead of "as well as", and make the verb plural ("were").

6. When a plural noun is the name for a single object, a singular verb is required.

"The Adventures of Marco Polo" were read by the class . . . INCORRECT.
"The Adventures of Marco Polo" was read by the class . . . CORRECT.

The noun "Adventures" is plural, but, as it is part of the title of a book (single object), we must use the singular verb ("was read").

Similarly,
The United States (one country) has declared war . . . . . CORRECT.

EXERCISES ON NOUNS
(Rules 1 — 6)

Correct the following sentences, and give reasons for your alterations:

1. The boy and his father is walking down the street.
2. Tom, and not his brothers, are to blame.
3. "Gulliver's Travels" describe some remarkable adventures.
4. The speed of the aeroplanes were amazing
5. The progress of the explorers were stopped by swamps.
6. Iron, as well as coal, were found in the hills.
7. The huge liner, with its attendant tugs, were entering the harbour.
8. The Duke of Wellington was a soldier and a statesman.
9. My sister she is in hospital.
10. The king, accompanied by fifty soldiers, were marching down the street.
11. A carriage and pair were sold at the auction sale.
12. Across the bridge walked two men — a sergeant and corporal.
13. "Tom Brown's School Days" give true pictures of school life.
14. From a distance was heard the angry shouts of the peasants.
15. Joyce, with her two cousins, are staying with us.
16. An account of our victories were published in the paper.

17. "Horses" are plural.
18. The lioness, and not her two cubs, have been fed by the keeper.
19. A bomber roaring overhead and an armoured car racing along the street reminds us of the nearness of war.
20. The rain it fell heavily during the night.

NOUNS

(Rules 7 — 14)

7. If a collective noun indicates a group regarded as one, the verb is singular. However, when we wish to indicate the individual members of the group, the verb is plural.

The crowd were a large one . . . INCORRECT.
The crowd was a large one . . . CORRECT.

We must use the singular verb "was," because we are thinking of the crowd as a single thing.

But,

The crowd was scattered in all directions . . . INCORRECT.
The crowd were scattered in all directions . . . CORRECT.

The plural verb "were scattered," is used, because we are thinking of the individuals acting separately.

8. A collective noun must be treated as either singular or plural throughout the sentence.

Since the committee controls such matters, we must abide by their decision . . . INCORRECT.
Since the committee controls such matters, we must abide by its decision . . . CORRECT.

Since we regard the collective noun "committee" as one group (as shown by the singular verb), we must use a singular pronoun ("its").

Note that some collective nouns may have a plural, e.g., "classes", "groups".

9. Two or more singular parts of a subject, joined by "either . . . or" or "neither . . . nor", require a singular verb.

Neither the boy nor his friend were in the room . . . . . .
INCORRECT.
Neither the boy nor his friend was in the room. CORRECT.

As "boy" and "friend" are both singular, and are joined by "neither . . . nor," the singular verb "was" must be used.

10. When two or more parts of the subject connected by "either . . . or" or "neither . . . nor" are different in person or number, or in both, the verb agrees with the part of the subject nearest to it.

Neither the cows nor the dog were found . . . INCORRECT.
Neither the cows nor the dog was found . . . CORRECT.

The singular verb "was found" is used, because it agrees with the nearer part of the subject, "dog".

Some authorities disagree with this rule. They maintain that the sentence should be recast in this way:

The cows were not found, nor was the dog.

What alteration would you make in the following incorrect sentence? Give your reasons.

Neither Jane nor I is fond of hiking . . . INCORRECT.

11. The following nouns require a plural verb:

annals, shears, bellows, tongs, statistics, suds, pincers, scissors, proceeds, premises (buildings), thanks, tweezers.

When we wish to emphasize the singular aspect of such words as "shears," "scissors," etc., the phrase "a pair of" is used. A singular verb must then be used.

A pair of scissors was used . . . CORRECT.

12. The following nouns require a singular verb:

news, gallows.

Ill news runs apace . . . CORRECT.
The gallows has been erected . . . CORRECT.

13. In nouns expressing a quantity or a number, the sign of the plural is often dispensed with, especially when they are preceded by numerals.

e.g., "sixty head of cattle", "four pair of shoes", "I weigh seven stone", "an eight-day clock", "a four-penny pie".

14. The verb "to be" should always agree with the subject, never with the complement.

> The raids on German transport centres was part of a well-laid plan . . . INCORRECT.
> The raids on German transport centres were part of a well-laid plan . . . CORRECT.

The plural verb "were" must be used, because the simple subject "raids" is plural.

EXERCISES ON NOUNS
(Rules 7 — 14)

Correct the following sentences, and give reasons for your alterations:

1. The flock of sheep were a large one.
2. Neither the table nor the chair were broken.
3. Either you or I are greatly mistaken.
4. These premises is very dirty.
5. The crew has mutinied and put their officers in irons.
6. Here are a pair of tongs.
7. The company has chosen the site for their new factory.
8. The news of the great victories have encouraged our people.
9. Tom's shears has been sharpened.
10. Neither Jean nor I are going to the carnival.
11. Mary's daily visits to the hospital was an example to her classmates.
12. This group of islands, far away from the mainland, are rarely visited by ships.
13. Neither the aeroplane nor its passengers was seen again.
14. Thanks was given to the men who had organized the concert.
15. The regiment has gone into their new quarters.
16. As the gang were suspicious of one another, the detective soon discovered the name of its leader.
17. These tweezers was bought at the chemist's shop.
18. My horse, Tim, is a three-years-old.
19. Either Joyce or I are to play in the team.
20. The antics of the clown was a delight to all.

ADJECTIVES
(Rules 1 — 5)

1. When two persons or things are compared, the comparative is used; when more than two, the superlative.

> He is the strongest of the two boys . . . INCORRECT.
> He is the stronger of the two boys . . . CORRECT.

This is the better of the three horses . . . INCORRECT.
This is the best of the three horses . . . CORRECT.

2. Double comparatives and double superlatives should be avoided.

You are more braver than I . . . INCORRECT.
You are braver than I . . . CORRECT.

3. Strictly speaking, there can be but "one first" and "one last".

I bought the three first pies in the shop . . . INCORRECT.
I bought the first three pies in the shop . . . CORRECT.

4. "Less" is always used of quantity; "fewer" always refers to number.

There were less people at the match today . . . INCORRECT.
There were fewer people at the match today . . . CORRECT.

Distinguish between "few" and "a few"; "little" and "a little". The first of each pair is negative in meaning; the second, positive.

5. Make sure that you say "this kind", "this sort".

Frequently we hear "These kind of apples is delicious". The noun "kind" (or "sort") requires a singular form—"this". The demonstratives "these" and "those" are plural.

This kind of apple is delicious . . . CORRECT.

EXERCISES ON ADJECTIVES
(Rules 1 — 5)

Rewrite the following sentences correctly, and state reasons for your alterations:

1. The youngest of the two girls is the happiest.
2. Our class obtained the three first places in the race.
3. These kind of mistakes is very costly.
4. Our full-back made less mistakes in Wednesday's match.
5. Mine is the more better book.
6. I like to walk on the shadiest side of the street.
7. Those kind of people are always in trouble.
8. It was the most unkindest remark I had ever heard.
9. Mary, Lucy and Jean are sitting in the three last seats in the circus.
10. A more happier day I never spent, although there were less prizes this year.

11. Of the two swimmers, the taller is the more stronger.
12. These sort of apples come from Tasmania.
13. I spent the two first days of the holidays in bed.
14. Of two evils, choose the least.
15. The more lonelier path led the three girls to a house around which there were less trees. Then Gwen said to June, "Take the largest of these two sticks, and strike the three first palings of the fence."

ADJECTIVES

(Rules 6 — 9)

6. Many adjectives do not properly admit of comparison, e.g.,

perfect, chief, unique, square, equal, dead, circular, heavenly, right, empty, full.

Why would it be incorrect to use any of the above words in either the comparative or the superlative degree?

7. Do not confuse "latter" and "last". "Latter" should be confined to the second of two things previously mentioned; "last" to the final of three or more things previously mentioned.

He brought pen and ink, the last in a small bottle . . . INCORRECT.
He brought pen and ink, the latter in a small bottle . . . CORRECT.
He brought pen, paper and ink, the latter in a small bottle . . . INCORRECT.
He brought pen, paper and ink, the last in a small bottle . . . CORRECT.

8. The distributive adjectives "each", "every", "either" and "neither" are singular, because they refer to each individual member of a group. They must, therefore, be followed by nouns and verbs in the singular. Even if two nouns qualified by distributive adjectives are joined by "and", the verb must still be singular; a singular verb is required by the marked singular effect of "each", "every", "either", or "neither".

Every horse and cow were sold . . . INCORRECT.
Every horse and cow was sold . . . CORRECT.

9. When a comparison is being made, "other" should be used after a comparative adjective.

Jimmy is taller than any boy in his class . . . INCORRECT.
Since "any boy" includes Jimmy, we are really stating that Jimmy is taller than himself.
Jimmy is taller than any other boy in his class . . . CORRECT.
(or) Jimmy is the tallest boy in his class . . . CORRECT.

EXERCISES ON ADJECTIVES

(Rules 6 — 9)

Wherever possible, correct the following sentences and give reasons for your alterations:

1. The Alsatian was more valuable than any dog in the show.
2. Cut that wood more square.
3. Every man and woman were saved.
4. It was the most unique offer ever made.
5. Each boy and girl have done their best.
6. My brothers, George, Tom and Jack attend school, the latter being the best scholar.
7. Each boy and girl were given a prize.
8. Montgomery was braver than any general of his time.
9. Every day and night were spent in hard work.
10. Tom is stronger than any boy in his club.
11. Your solution of the problem is more correct.
12. Every man and boy were ready to fight.
13. My bottle of ginger beer is emptier than yours.
14. Ingram is wealthier than any man in his town.
15. The diamond was a most matchless specimen.

PRONOUNS

(Rules 1 — 5)

1. A singular pronoun must not be used to refer to a plural noun or vice versa.

This aeroplane is the fastest in the world. They are now being produced in great numbers . . . INCORRECT.
This aeroplane is the fastest in the world. It is now being produced in great numbers . . . CORRECT.

2. The pronoun "you" is always coupled with a plural verb, even when it is used instead of the name of one person.

Was you anxious to come, Tom? . . . INCORRECT.
Were you anxious to come, Tom? . . . CORRECT.

3. "All" is usually plural, but is singular when it means "everything".

All is well at home.

This sentence is correct, if "all" means "everything"; but, if we are referring to the members of the family, we must use "are".

4. Do not use an emphatic pronoun as the subject of a verb.

My brother and myself hope to gain prizes . . . INCORRECT.

Probably modesty has caused the substitution of "myself" for the correct pronoun "I".

Some authorities argue in this way: the emphatic pronoun "myself", though seemingly in apposition to a nominative personal pronoun, is really in the objective case, some preposition, such as "for", being understood.

My brother and I hope to gain prizes . . . CORRECT.

5. When pronouns of different persons are used, place them in this order: Third, Second, First.

You, I and Jean are invited . . . INCORRECT.
Jean, you and I are invited . . . CORRECT.

EXERCISES ON PRONOUNS
(Rules 1 — 5)

Wherever possible, correct the following sentences and give reasons for your alterations:

1. If I and he ever meet, there will be trouble.
2. All who went to the party seems to have enjoyed it.
3. Although opossums are protected by law, he is still hunted for his skin.
4. They told Ned that you was going, Joe.
5. You, I and she should enjoy ourselves at the picnic.
6. She spoke to me and you.
7. He has written his novel, but they will not be on sale for some time.

8. The ship was carrying a valuable cargo, but unfortunately all were ruined.
9. My friend and myself hope to do well in business.
10. We knew that this boy and yourself started the fire.
11. I could not understand why you was not present.
12. Our enemies who thought that aeroplanes would bring them victory are now finding it the first cause of their ruin.
13. The arrested man told his story, but, as himself well knew, it was difficult to believe.
14. All who have seen it tells the same story.
15. The secretary said that you was resigning from the club.

PRONOUNS
(Rules 6 — 10)

6. A pronoun should have a clear subject of reference.

> John accompanied Tom to Sydney where he bought a rifle . . . INCORRECT.

This sentence does not indicate clearly who bought the rifle. Therefore, remodel it:

> John went with Tom to Sydney and there bought a rifle . . . CORRECT.
> Similarly,
> Several trains were cancelled, and it caused great inconvenience . . . INCORRECT.

In this sentence "it" has no clear subject of reference. Therefore, recast the sentence:

> The cancellation of several trains caused great inconvenience . . . CORRECT.

7. Care must be taken when "who" and "whom" are used as interrogative pronouns.

> Whom do you think they were? . . . INCORRECT.

As the interrogative pronoun is the complement of "were", "who" must be used instead of "whom".

Why is it incorrect to use "who" in the following sentence?

> Who did you see at the pictures? . . . INCORRECT.

8. When the verb is omitted in adverbial clauses of comparison after the conjunction "as" and "than", the case of the pronoun must be determined by supplying the understood verb.

> Jean is taller than me . . . INCORRECT.

By supplying the understood verb "am," we can see the fault.

Jean is taller than I . . . CORRECT.

Can you explain how the following correct sentences differ in meaning?

You blamed him as much as I.

You blamed him as much as me.

9. The pronouns "anybody", "nobody", "everybody", "each", "either", and "neither" when used in the subject, require to be followed by a singular verb and a singular pronoun.

Everybody were present . . . INCORRECT.

Everybody was present . . . CORRECT.

Everybody was busy in their gardens . . . INCORRECT.

Everybody was busy in his garden . . . CORRECT.

Since "everybody" is singular, we must use "his" (or "her").

Look at these sentences:

The boys and girls were nervous, but each was determined to do his best . . .INCORRECT.

The boys and girls were nervous, but all were determined to do their best . . . CORRECT.

Can you justify the recasting of the sentence?

10. "Either" is used for two things; "any one" for more than two.

Either of these three girls would make a good prefect . . . INCORRECT.

Any one of these three girls would make a good prefect . . . CORRECT.

What is the distinction between "anyone" and "any one" in the following sentences?

Anyone is liable to make a mistake.

Any one of us is liable to make a mistake.

EXERCISES ON PRONOUNS

(Rules 6 — 10)

Wherever possible, correct the following sentences, and give reasons for your corrections:

1. Who were you thinking of when you said that?
2. He told his father that he had broken the window.

3. You did not study as much as me.
4. Neither of these suggestions seem pleasant to him.
5. In that team were seven good batsmen, either of whom were capable of making a century.
6. Whom did you say he is?
7. Although I worked as hard as Keith, you paid him more than I.
8. Nobody should neglect their pets when they go on holidays.
9. As Tom and I were both guilty, father punished him as much as I.
10. There were two candidates, but I did not approve of any one of them.
11. Tom did not say good-bye to his friend before he left.
12. Anybody who held their land direct from the king were members of this council.
13. Any one would buy anyone of these two puppies.
14. Judith plays a better game than him.
15. Five men and three women were brought before the tribunal, and each knew that he could expect no mercy.

PRONOUNS

(Rules 11 — 14)

11. A relative pronoun should be placed as near as possible to its antecedent.

> The king visited the airmen's quarters, who had just returned from a raid . . . INCORRECT.

The adjectival clause qualifies "airmen"; therefore, bring them together:

> The king visited the quarters of the airmen, who had just returned from a raid . . . CORRECT.

Similarly,

> Stories have often been related about these islands, which are absolutely ridiculous . . . INCORRECT.

> Stories, which are absolutely ridiculous, have often been related about these islands . . . CORRECT.

12. A relative pronoun agrees with its antecedent in person and number, but takes its case from its own clause.

> I am the boy who they have chosen for the position . . . INCORRECT.

The relative pronoun should be in the objective case,

governed by the verb "have chosen"; its form, therefore, should be "whom."

> I am the boy whom they have chosen for the position . . .
> CORRECT.

Can you justify the following alteration?

INCORRECT	CORRECT
It was one of those balls that **tempts** a batsman to take a risk.	**TEMPT**

13. The relative pronoun "which" should not be used to refer to a whole clause.

> He killed the snake, which greatly pleased the girls . . .
> INCORRECT.

As there is no noun or noun-equivalent acting as an antecedent to "which", the sentence should be reconstructed.

> By killing the snake, he greatly pleased the girls . . .
> CORRECT.

14. Exercise care with a relative pronoun before a parenthesis.

> The police are anxious to interview a man whom, they know, was a friend of the victim . . . INCORRECT.

The relative pronoun should be in the nominative case to the verb "was". Therefore, we should use "who" in this sentence.

> The police are anxious to interview a man who, they know, was a friend of the victim . . . CORRECT.

INVESTIGATION EXERCISES

Can you justify the following alterations?

INCORRECT	CORRECT
There are many people ∧ say the contrary.	WHO
I hear you have bought a car. I hope you are pleased with **same.**	∧ IT
One should take care of **his** books.	ONE'S

EXERCISES ON PRONOUNS
(Rules 11 — 14)

Wherever possible, correct the following sentences, and give reasons for your corrections:

1. We visited the convicts' graves who had been killed by the blacks.
2. Your complaint has been noted, and inquiries are being made with regard to same.
3. This attack is one of the most treacherous acts that has ever been committed.
4. One should read widely to improve his knowledge of English.
5. The old man's clothes who had sought shelter from the rain, were torn and dirty.
6. There are boys whom, I believe, read grammar books for pleasure.
7. He is one of those people who never worries.
8. As I flew over the desert, I marvelled at their courage who had first crossed it on foot.
9. He commenced to sing, which annoyed me extremely.
10. She is the girl who we have nominated to represent the school.
11. The youth smiled at the girl, which caused her to blush.
12. He was a player whom, all maintained, would never question the umpire's decision.
13. Information has been obtained about the stolen money which would be helpful to the police.
14. Thelma is one of those girls who plays tennis every day.
15. Churchill is the man whom, the world knows, inspired Britain.

VERBS
(Rules 1 — 5)

1. Transitive verbs govern nouns and noun equivalents in the objective case.

The dog followed Harry and I . . . INCORRECT.

Since the transitive verb "followed" governs the pronoun in the objective case, "I" should be changed to "me".

The dog followed Harry and me . . . CORRECT.

2. The verb "to be" takes the same case after it as before it.

It was him . . . INCORRECT.

Both pronouns should be in the nominative case. "Him" is incorrect, since it is in the objective case.

It was he . . . CORRECT.

Why is the following sentence correct?

I recognized that boy to be him.

3. "Can" denotes ability; "may" seeks permission.

"Can I eat this slice of melon?" said the fat boy . . . INCORRECT.

Here the speaker is certainly asking for permission; hence, "can" should be changed to "may."

"May I eat this slice of melon?" said the fat boy . . . CORRECT.

4. Remember that the teacher teaches, the pupil learns.

My father learnt Tom to play football . . . INCORRECT.
My father taught Tom to play football . . . CORRECT.

5. Do not use a past participle for a past tense, or a past tense for a past participle.

He swum across the river . . . INCORRECT.

The correct form of the past tense is "swam." "Swum" is the past participle.

He swam across the river . . . CORRECT.

What alteration would you make in the following sentence?

Has she showed you her prizes? . . . INCORRECT.

Note.—

The student should make a careful study of **Verbs and Their Principal Parts, pages 61-64.**

EXERCISES ON VERBS

(Rules 1 — 5)

Wherever possible, correct the following sentences, and give the reasons for your corrections:

1. "Can I ask a question?" said a man standing at the back of the hall.
2. I thought that it might have been her.
3. The current swept my friend and I close to the rocks.
4. I wish you would learn me how to play that stroke.

5. Tommy has sawed the leg off the chair.
6. Can I see your ticket, please?
7. This book will learn you how to write a composition.
8. The small boy rung the door-bell and then raced round the corner.
9. We saw Harold and he hurrying to the station.
10. Can I take Beryl to the pictures?
11. He sprung upon the horse and galloped across the draw-bridge.
12. We knew at once that it was them.
13. We left Mary and she playing tennis.
14. After he had rode many weary miles, the traveller came to a river.
15. It is him whom the police suspect.

VERBS

(Rules 6 — 10)

6. "Has got" means "has obtained" or "has captured"; "has" denotes simple possession.

The panther has got a shiny, black coat . . . INCORRECT.

In this sentence simple possession should have been indicated; hence, "has" should be used.

The panther has a shiny, black coat . . . CORRECT.

Can you explain why the following sentence is correct?

They have got gold from the mine.

7. When two auxiliaries are used with one principal verb, the principal verb need not be repeated, if the same form will do for both. If, however, one form will not do for both, two forms must be given, one for each auxiliary.

He never has, and never will hurt anyone's feelings . . . CORRECT.

This is correct, because we can say "He never has hurt" and "He never will hurt."

But,

He never has, and never will see a black tiger . . . INCORRECT.

We cannot say, "He never has see"; we must say "He never has seen."

He never has seen, and never will see a black tiger . . . CORRECT.

8. If two verbs are used, the auxiliary of the second verb must be written, if the second verb is not the same as the first verb in number or voice.

Two warships were sunk and one damaged . . . INCORRECT.

The subject "one" requires a singular verb—"was damaged."

Two warships were sunk and one was damaged . . . CORRECT.

Note the number and voice of the verbs in the following sentence. Why is the sentence incorrect?

Two enemy generals have surrendered and one wounded . . . INCORRECT.

9. Make sure that a participial expression has a clear subject of reference.

Coming home, the storm caused a delay . . . INCORRECT.

It was not the *storm* that was coming home; it was a *person* or *persons*. We must, therefore, reconstruct the sentence so that the participle qualifies a suitable noun or pronoun.

Coming home, we were delayed by the storm . . . CORRECT.

10. A noun or pronoun used before a gerund must be in the possessive, not in the objective case.

My father disliked me leaving school . . . INCORRECT.

My father did not dislike "me"; he disliked my action —*my leaving school.*

Therefore,

My father disliked my leaving school . . . CORRECT.

Similarly,

On entering the hall, the noise was deafening . . . IN-CORRECT.

Since a person, not a noise, was entering the hall, we must insert before "entering" a noun or pronoun in the possessive case.

On his entering the hall, the noise was deafening . . . CORRECT.

How do the following correct sentences differ in meaning?

> The difficulty will be overcome by the agent's going to Sydney.
>
> The difficulty will be overcome by the agent going to Sydney.

EXERCISES ON VERBS

(Rules 6 — 10)

Wherever possible, correct the following sentences, and give reasons for your corrections.

1. Having worked hard during the year, the examination seemed easy.
2. I look forward to the time when he will do as much for me as I have for him.
3. "Grandma, what strong, white teeth you've got!" said Red Riding Hood
4. Will you overlook me being late for the party?
5. One passenger was killed and several injured in an accident to a suburban train
6. All the evidence points to the fact that he has and is working still for a foreign government.
7. Have you got any fruit in your bag?
8. On arriving at the scene of the accident, the body was being taken away in an ambulance.
9. England always has, and always will, produce great men in her hour of need
10. The area was divided into sectors, and the sectors placed under the control of wardens.
11. Through missing the train the dinner was late.
12. Arriving at the station, the train had just left.
13. The girl, who is sitting opposite to us, has got an attractive smile.
14. We hope that you will work as hard for us as you have for them.
15. The train continued on its journey without Harold realizing that he was being overcarried.
16. This firm has been established in Sydney in the last thirty years, and opened several branches in the country
17. Being the lunch hour, we strolled into the park.
18. A broken leg prevented him chasing the burglar.
19. When the launch sank, two men were drowned and one saved.
20. Without another word, the innkeeper left the room, and shouting to someone in the yard below, the horses were soon brought round to the door.

VERBS

(Rules 11 — 14)

11. If the simple future tense of the verb is required, use "shall" for the first person and "will" for the second and third.

12. If something more than futurity is meant, e.g., determination, a command, a promise, or a threat, "will" is used in the first person and "shall" in the second and third.

I will do this in spite of your opposition . . . CORRECT.

Because determination, as well as futurity, is meant, "will do" is correct.

Why are the following sentences correct?

You shall hear from me without fail.

Tom shall not go to the pictures unless his work is finished.

13. Generally speaking, a past tense in the principal clause is followed by a past tense in the subordinate clause.

I came (*or* had come) so that I may help you . . . INCORRECT.

The past tense "came" in the principal clause requires a past tense in the subordinate clause; hence, "might help" should be used instead of "may help."

I came (*or* had come) so that I might help you . . . CORRECT.

There are two important exceptions to this rule:

(*a*) If the subordinate clause states an action that is universally or habitually true, the present tense should be used in that clause.

I was taught (Past) that swimming is good (Present) for correct breathing . . . CORRECT.

He asked (Past) me why I train (Present) at the oval every day . . . CORRECT.

(*b*) If the subordinate clause is a comparison clause, any tense can be used in that clause.

He loved me more than he loves (*or* will love *or* loved) you . . . CORRECT.

14. Generally speaking, a present or future tense in the principal clause is followed by any tense in the subordinate clause, according to the sense required.

Exception:

To express purpose in the subordinate clause "may" must be used, if the verb in the principal clause is present, perfect, or future tense.

> He works (*or* has worked *or* will work) very hard so that he may succeed . . . CORRECT.

As the verb "works" in the principal clause is present tense, "may succeed" is correctly used in the subordinate clause expressing purpose.

EXERCISES ON VERBS

(Rules 11 — 14)

Wherever possible, correct the following sentences, and give reasons for your corrections:

1. We hope that you might be able to come to the dance.
2. I will most likely see him to-morrow.
3. These trees are being cut down so that a road might be constructed.
4. We shall have our way in spite of your opposition.
5. I was taught at school that fresh air and sunlight developed a healthy body.
6. The king shall return from North Africa by a secret route.
7. We shall send them a sample of this paper so that they might be able to judge its quality.
8. You shall, I think, hear from him shortly.
9. The court martial will have decided by to-morrow whether he might be released.
10. Who was the first to discover that the world was round?
11. Our parents had agreed that we may go to the zoo.
12. We will, I believe, finish the work on time.
13. Was it Harvey who discovered how the blood circulated?
14. Your parents have made these sacrifices in order that you might have your chance in life.
15. We were saving our money so that we may buy mother a present.

ADVERBS

1. Do not confuse adjectives with adverbs.

Come quick . . . INCORRECT.

As the verb "come" requires an adverb, "quickly" (adverb) should be used instead of "quick" (adjective).

Come quickly . . . CORRECT.

Similarly,

You must fight more vigorous . . . INCORRECT.
You must fight more vigorously . . . CORRECT.

Study carefully the following sentences. Both are correct, but note how they differ in meaning:

(*a*) She looked foolish under the bed.
(*b*) She foolishly looked under the bed.

In (*a*) we use the adjective "foolish," because we mean "she looked a foolish person under the bed"; in (*b*) the adverb "foolishly" is used because we mean "she acted foolishly in looking under the bed."

2. Remember that adverbs of degree modify adjectives and other adverbs.

He was easy first in the race . . . INCORRECT.

If this were allowable, "easy" would be an adverb of degree modifying "first." "Easy," however, is an adjectival form; the adverbial form is "easily."

He was easily first in the race . . . CORRECT.

Similarly,

Jean writes remarkable well . . . INCORRECT.
Jean writes remarkably well . . . CORRECT.

3. Always observe the combination "so . . . that".

I was that hungry that I could not wait for you . . . INCORRECT.

If this were permissible, "that" would be an adverb of degree modifying the adjective "hungry." "That" is never an adverb. The correct word is "so."

I was so hungry that I could not wait for you . . . CORRECT.

4. Avoid the double negative, unless you wish to state a mild affirmative.

I did not say nothing . . . INCORRECT.
I did not say anything . . . CORRECT.

In the first sentence, the two negatives make an affirmative. The meaning of the sentence is different, therefore, from that intended.

He was not altogether inattentive . . . CORRECT (MILD AFFIRMATIVE).

5. "Hardly" and "scarcely" should not be used with negatives.

He is so fat that he cannot hardly run . . . INCORRECT.

This sentence is absurd, because it combines in one idea (1) an impossibility, (2) a partial possibility.

He is so fat that he can hardly run . . . CORRECT.

6. "Hardly" and "scarcely" should be followed by "when" or "before", never by "than".

He had hardly entered the jungle . . .

This should be followed by a "time clause." The correct word to introduce this time clause is "when." We cannot use "than" because it commences a comparison clause.

INVESTIGATION EXERCISES

Can you justify the following alterations?

INCORRECT	CORRECT
Directly he comes, I shall tell you.	AS SOON AS
He was captured after by the Indians.	AFTERWARDS
England and Scotland were united together.	Omit "TOGETHER"
I never brought my lunch today.	DID NOT BRING
I dislike cold worse than heat.	MORE
I like football more than cricket.	BETTER

EXERCISES ON ADVERBS

Comment on the following sentences and correct them:

1. The morning was that cold that we did not like getting out of bed.
2. I was real sorry for you.
3. Soon after a shot was fired.
4. Do you like chocolates more than ice-cream?
5. Don't walk so slow.
6. I shall never reveal your secret to nobody.
7. We had scarcely entered the house than the rain came down in torrents.
8. Some people act very stupid when they drink alcohol.
9. I detest him worse than I detest her.
10. They were miserable poor.
11. The lion fought fiercer than ever.
12. Do not show him none of your books.
13. Hardly had he spoken than a shot was fired.
14. Directly he comes to the house, show him your dog.
15. Tom batted too careful in the match.
16. Shortly after lightning struck the tree.
17. Mary sang sweeter at this concert.
18. The rain fell that heavy that we could not scarcely see the game.
19. Unless you speak more distinct, the audience will not hear you.
20. The clown was that funny that all the people could scarcely stop laughing. "He was real good," said Tom. "Yes," said Heather, "I liked him more than last year's clown. He was that comical that I couldn't eat no chocolates until he returned again to the dressing room."

PREPOSITIONS

(Rules 1 — 5)

1. Prepositions should be followed by nouns or pronouns in the objective case.

He went with you and I . . . INCORRECT.

The preposition "with" governs both pronouns in the objective case. "I" is in the nominative case; "me" is in the objective case.

He went with you and me . . . CORRECT.

Similarly,

We said it was for he and she . . . INCORRECT.
We said it was for him and her . . . CORRECT.

2. As a general rule, "between" is used with reference to two things; "among" or "amongst" with reference to three or more things.

> He distributed ten pounds between the four boys . . . INCORRECT.
>
> He distributed ten pounds among the four boys . . . CORRECT.
>
> A friendly feeling developed among England and America . . . INCORRECT.
>
> A friendly feeling developed between England and America . . . . CORRECT.

3. Do not confuse "beside" with "besides". "Beside" means "by the side of", and hence sometimes "outside of"; "besides" means "in addition to".

> He sat beside me . . . CORRECT (near me).
>
> Your answer is beside the question . . . CORRECT (irrelevant to the question).
>
> Besides giving advice, I gave practical assistance . . . CORRECT (in addition to).

4. Do not insert unnecessary prepositions.

> The young boys crossed over the Pacific . . . INCORRECT.
> The young boys crossed the Pacific . . . CORRECT.
>
> The regiment descended down the hill . . . INCORRECT.
> The regiment descended the hill . . . CORRECT.

It will be noticed that in each incorrect sentence the meaning of the preposition has already been expressed in the verb. Therefore, the preposition is not required.

5. Do not omit necessary prepositions. Certain words require particular prepositions.

> e.g.,

INCORRECT	CORRECT
They prevented me ∧ going.	FROM
Your action admits ∧ no excuse.	OF

EXERCISES ON PREPOSITIONS
(Rules 1 — 5)

Rewrite the following sentences correctly and justify your alterations:

1. The snake reared up its head.
2. I wrote you last night to find out who you gave that letter to.
3. The water-mill besides the stream is working well.
4. The two robber-chiefs divided the booty between all the members of their gangs.
5. Beside clothing, food was given to the old man, who had ascended up the hill.
6. Between the races of Africa there is little unity.
7. Who did you serve under in the Cadets?
8. The ruffians hindered me going to my home.
9. Where have you been to?
10. When I was walking besides the river, I saw an alligator lying between the reeds.
11. He laid the blame upon somebody, I know not who, in the company.
12. For why did you do that?
13. They discouraged me taking the apples home, so I divided them among Jean and Lola.
14. Who has been operated for appendicitis?
15. They were awarded with medals.

PREPOSITIONS
(Rules 6 — 10)

6. Use the correct prepositions after certain nouns, adjectives and verbs. You should study carefully the section on Prepositional Idioms (pages 64-67).

Here are some common mistakes:

INCORRECT	CORRECT
This change is **to** the better.	**FOR**
We profit **from** experience.	**BY**
That is different **to** mine.	**FROM**
The crown is adorned **by** gems.	**WITH**

7. Although, generally speaking, it is inadvisable to end a sentence with a preposition, no definite rule can be followed. If the preposition "sounds comfortable" (Fowler's Modern English Usage) at the end of the sentence, use it. Every person must be his own judge.

Which of the following would you alter? Why?

(a) Whom did you ask for?
(b) He disliked being laughed at.
(c) This is the book I spoke of.
(d) Which street is your house in?
(e) What did they dig the field we used to play cricket in up for?

8. If two or more words requiring different prepositions are used in the same sentence, the different prepositions should be written.

I disagree and object to your decision . . . INCORRECT.

The verb "disagree" requires the preposition "with." Therefore,

I disagree with, and object to your decision . . . CORRECT.

9. Do not confuse "without" or "except" with "unless". Generally speaking, "without" and "except" are prepositions; their use as conjunctions is inadvisable.

I cannot go without I obtain permission . . . INCORRECT.

The two ideas "I cannot go" and "I obtain permission," require a conjunction. "Unless" is preferred to "without," which is a colloquial conjunction.

I cannot go unless I obtain permission . . . CORRECT.
Similarly,

You will fail except you follow my advice . . . INCORRECT.

You will fail unless you follow my advice . . . CORRECT.

10. Avoid the expression "as to".

I doubt as to the truth of your statement . . . INCORRECT.

The verb "doubt" must have a direct object—a noun, a pronoun or a noun clause. In this sentence the direct object is "truth."

I doubt the truth of your statement . . . CORRECT.

The same reasoning applies to:

My brother decides as to whether I may go . . . INCORRECT.
My brother decides whether I may go . . . CORRECT.

"As to" is sometimes used as a slovenly substitute for a simple preposition, e.g.,

INCORRECT	CORRECT
She was very sarcastic **as to** his dress.	**ABOUT**
Every detail **as to** the work has been arranged.	**CONCERNING**

EXERCISES ON PREPOSITIONS
(Rules 6 — 10)

Make necessary alterations in the following sentences and justify your corrections:

1. You must decide as to when we depart.
2. Who does this dog belong to?
3. The injured man was carried by a stretcher to the hospital.
4. Except you run, you will not catch the train.
5. Our captain made changes and additions to the team.
6. What are they going to pave the street that your house is in with?
7. The twins bore no resemblance with each other.
8. Though I am not in agreement, I was much impressed by your statement.
9. My sister cannot arrive in time for the picnic without she comes by a motor car.
10. I leave it to you to decide as to whether we stay or depart from this camp.
11. The pirates tried to take the vessel off us.
12. I know who you learned who this pen-knife belongs to from.
13. Without you come on the fox-hunt, I shall not go because I can seldom hit the mark I aim for.
14. We are not eligible to this club, because we have not complied with the regulations.
15. Without our footballers train more thoroughly they will be defeated at many games.

CONJUNCTIONS
(Rules 1 — 5)

1. Avoid the use of "reason why . . . because".

The reason why he did not come was because he had no
money . . . INCORRECT.

The word "because" unnecessarily repeats the idea
conveyed by "reason why." Therefore,

The reason why he did not come was that he had no money
. . . CORRECT.

(or) He did not come because he had no money . . .
CORRECT.

2. Do not confuse "providing" with "provided".

We use "provided" as a conjunction when a stipulation
is expressed. It is an abbreviated form of "it being provided."
"Providing" cannot express this meaning.

Providing you come with us, we shall enjoy ourselves . . .
INCORRECT.

Provided you come with us, we shall enjoy ourselves . . .
CORRECT.

3. Both the conjunctions "as" and "than" must be included in a double comparative sentence.

A lion is as powerful, if not more powerful, than a tiger . . .
INCORRECT.

We cannot say, "A lion is as powerful than a tiger";
we must use the conjunction "as."

A lion is as powerful as, if not more powerful than, a tiger
. . . CORRECT.

Similarly,

You are as slow, or slower than a tortoise . . . INCORRECT.
You are as slow as, or slower than a tortoise . . . CORRECT.

4. Do not use "and which" unless a "which" clause precedes these two words.

I saw the seals swimming in the pool and which were making
queer noises . . . INCORRECT.

The conjunction "and" joins like clauses; therefore, it
should join here an adjectival clause to an adjectival clause.

I saw the seals which were swimming in the pool and which were making queer noises . . . CORRECT.

In the correct sentence "which were" of the second adjectival clause may be omitted, although the two words are understood.

I saw the seals which were swimming in the pool and making queer noises . . . CORRECT.

5. Make certain that you preserve the combination of the following "double harness" words.

EITHER . . . OR	I like either tea or cocoa.
NEITHER . . . NOR	He would take neither tea nor cocoa.
THOUGH . . . YET	Though we had plenty of blankets, yet George would not go camping with us.
WHETHER . . . OR	I do not know whether to laugh or cry.
SUCH . . . THAT	Such was her persistence that the work was finished before ten o'clock.
NO SOONER . . . THAN	No sooner did I receive the message than I hurried to your place.
BOTH . . . AND	Both Shirley and Jean are coming.

EXERCISES ON CONJUNCTIONS

(Rules 1 — 5)

Rewrite the following sentences correctly and state your reasons for alterations:

1. The animal with a striped skin, and which is like a big cat, is called a tiger.
2. This team is as good, if not better than the one we had last year.
3. You are not lazy nor careless.
4. The reason why the men advanced was because they were inspired by their leader.
5. No sooner she had gone I found her watch.
6. The lion will be caught, providing our natives do not desert us.
7. My cricket bat is not better, and not even as good as yours.
8. I have neither gold or silver.
9. I came to a house built on the top of a hill and which was owned by a queer old man.

10. The explanation of our defeat is because we did not train.
11. No sooner did she receive the message but she left the farm.
12. On the platform were several men stern in appearance but who were kind to the children.
13. Providing he returns the watch, no action will be taken against him.
14. My reason for taking her part was because she had always been my friend.
15. My bad-tempered cousin would neither play in our hockey team or accompany us to the baths.
16. Providing the weather is fine, the picnic will be held.

CONJUNCTIONS

(Rules 6 — 9)

6. "Like" must never be used as a conjunction.

It can be used as a prepositional adjective, e.g.,
Tom was like (similar to) me.
or as a prepositional adverb, e.g.,
He talks like (similarly to) an expert.
He fought like you would have fought . . . INCORRECT.
Since the second clause is a "manner clause," it should commence with "as."
He fought as you would have fought . . . CORRECT.
Observe that "like as" is sometimes used in sentences where "as" alone would express the meaning:
It looks like as if it is going to rain . . . INCORRECT.
It looks as if it is going to rain . . . CORRECT.

7. Do not use "was when".

The finest example of his bravery was when he defeated six of his enemies . . . INCORRECT.
The verb "was" should be followed by a noun-equivalent, not by an adverbial clause.
The finest example of his bravery was his defeat of six of his enemies . . . CORRECT.
It is possible to use "when" (but not "was when") by recasting the sentence:
The finest example of his bravery was seen when he defeated six of his enemies . . . CORRECT.

8. The adverb "now" should not be used as a conjunction, unless it is accompanied by "that".

Now she has arrived, we shall go . . . INCORRECT.
Now that she has arrived, we shall go . . . CORRECT.

9. Do not use "also" as a co-ordinating conjunction.

To-day I was sowing wheat, also I was repairing the fence . . . INCORRECT.

Since "also" is an adverb, it cannot join clauses,
To-day I was sowing wheat, and also (I was) repairing the fence . . . CORRECT.
Similarly,
Nancy was tired, also hungry . . . INCORRECT.

Nancy was tired $\left\{ \begin{array}{c} \text{and} \\ \text{as well as} \end{array} \right\}$ hungry . . . CORRECT.

INVESTIGATION EXERCISES

Can you justify the following corrections?

INCORRECT	CORRECT
I knew <u>as</u> she was wrong.	**THAT**
Be sure <u>and</u> ask him.	**TO**
He is so weak I doubt <u>that</u> he can walk.	**WHETHER**
She has no other purpose <u>but</u> to help us.	**THAN**
It will be a long time <u>till</u> he goes there again.	**BEFORE**
He represented himself ∧ a poor man.	**AS**
	∧

EXERCISES ON CONJUNCTIONS

(Rules 6 — 9 and Investigation Exercises)

Rewrite the following sentences correctly and state your reasons for alterations:

1. Now it has stopped raining, we shall go.
2. The old man hurried along the mountain path just like he did when he was young.
3. Remember and bring home some fruit.
4. Your rashness makes me doubt that you are right.
5. Tom's best achievement was when he kicked a goal from the half-way mark.
6. Try and come with us now the sun is shining.
7. The orchardist watched me like a cat watches a mouse once it comes into a room.

8. I never heard as she was ill.

9. I have chopped the wood, also I have helped Bert to prepare the fire.

10. We should win more matches now we have a good coach.

11. They will be trapped like their comrades in the jungle were.

12. One of England's greatest sea exploits was when she smashed the Italian Fleet near Cape Matapan.

13. He bats like his brother does.

14. Now he has returned to his home-country, also gathered his followers, he has no other object but to fight against the invaders.

15. Her speech was too long, also too difficult to hear.

THE USE OF "ONLY"

Unless "only" is put in its correct place in a sentence, a meaning different from that intended may be conveyed.

Look at these sentences:

Only he sang this evening at eight.= *He, and no one else sang.*
He only sang this evening at eight.= *He sang, but did not do anything else.*
He sang only this evening at eight.= *He sang this evening, but not on any other occasion.*
He sang this evening only at eight.= *He sang at eight o'clock, but at no other time.*

EXERCISES ON "ONLY"

Insert "only" in different positions in the following sentences. How many sentences can you compose? How do they differ in meaning?

1. Girls may play vigoro.

2. Tom met my cousin.

3. To-day the boys were playing on the cricket field.

4. Joyce gave me two shillings.

5. My brother bought a bicycle at Christmas time.

AMBIGUOUS SENTENCES

An ambiguous sentence has more than one meaning. In the following, explain (*a*) what the unintentional meaning is, (*b*) what the true meaning is. Rewrite each sentence so that no ambiguity exists.

1. The judge told the prisoner that he was the biggest liar in the court.
2. This powder is used by the owners of dogs to kill their fleas.
3. I do not intend to leave you because you won first prize in the Lottery.
4. Don't go elsewhere to be swindled; come in here.
5. The native woman had to brush, dust, cook and wash her baby every day.
6. The owners of some factories do not care how their workmen live so long as they become rich.
7. The king should not wear clothes to distinguish him from his people.
8. When I advocated abolition of night-work for girls, my sister said that she was in favour of it.
9. Our science teacher's next experiment was not the least interesting.
10. I meant nothing less than to cause you annoyance.
11. Don't kill your wife with work; let electricity do it.
12. An umbrella was lost by a woman with silver ribs.
13. If fresh apple is not digested by the child, cook it.
14. George told his brother he had won the prize.
15. Bring the football in any case.
16. The supper was served in the large girls' room.
17. Susie loves her mother more than Joan.
18. I was pleased to see his last picture.
19. I shall spend my vacation shooting at my country home.
20. Ask how old Mr. Hawkins is.
21. The flowers in the church are taken to those who are ill after the service.
22. Corporal punishment should be restricted to parents.
23. Do you believe him younger than I?
24. The building caught fire and the occupants sought safety in their pyjamas.
25. The young farmer soon learnt to breed better pigs than his father.
26. This is our fourth child named Tom.
27. Examine our goods before you buy; you won't regret it.
28. The firemen only fought the flames for one hour, but in that time great damage was done.
29. The rebels entered the city, and captured the king who was in bed, together with fifty of his followers.
30. These shoes are very fashionable; some men will wear nothing else.

REVISION SENTENCES

Explain and correct the errors in the following sentences:

Revision Group 1

1. Joan and I am cousins.
2. There seems to be less boys than girls in the water.
3. The lion rushed at the hunter, and he killed him.
4. The boy asked his sister to talk softer.
5. Can I help you and she to carry those parcels?
6. You cannot run in the final without you win your heat.
7. In the centre of the room was a little boy and girl.
8. George was that angry that he could not scarcely talk.
9. A variety of delicious cakes were divided between Joyce, Shirley and June.
10. Hurrying around the corner, the clock in the tower began to chime.
11. The clown, as well as the children, seem to be enjoying the fun.
12. He said that you was to remain here until he returned.
13 Now we have rode all this distance, can we swim in the river?
14. Joyce is the prettier of the three girls, but not the stronger.
15. Poe's "Tales of Mystery" are very exciting.
16. If you hold the bat like I learnt you, you will play that stroke easier.
17 Compare this against that and you will be astonished with the result.
18. I do not like those sort of hats.
19. We had hardly put the ferret into the burrow than a rabbit scampered out.
20. Since you have got less chairs than me, we will hold the cricket meeting in my house.
21. Every man, woman and child were startled by the two first reports from the gun.
22. We have, and I hope, always will be friends.
23. As a result of the inquiry two men were dismissed and one disrated.
24 During the service grandfather began to snore, which caused everybody to look in our direction.
25 We heard after that he had scarcely done nothing to help us.
26. A number of lifebelts were distributed between the passengers, and scarcely was this task completed than a violent explosion occurred.
27. As we were being showed over the old convict ship, we thought of their suffering, who had sailed in her.
28. You cannot have this chocolate without you pay for it.
29. I prefer swimming more than diving.
30. Those kind of men cannot help you like I do.

Revision Group 2

1. When my uncle died, his farm, as well as his cattle, were sold.
2. At some distance from the shore was seen the grey shapes of several warships.
3. I asked three people the way to the post office, but neither of them were able to tell me.
4. Neither Jean or I are going to the city for the three last days of our vacation.
5. Providing you behave yourself, you might come with us.
6. Harold has killed more snakes than any man in the country.
7. The hermit has not moved from his place of lonely isolation.
8. On going to the front door, the little boy had run away.
9. The reason I bought this car is because it is easy to get parts for them.
10. It looks like as if our troops are going to cross over the desert.
11. I advise you to consult this doctor whom, I feel sure, will cure you.
12. This is one of those situations that requires a cool head.
13. The children were that noisy that the audience could not scarcely hear the actor's words.
14. The climate of this country is as good as England.
15. The boys, not noticing that the owner of the orchard was coming, they continued to pick the fruit.
16. The brig had no sooner rounded the point when several canoes were seen.
17. He is one of the few players who has scored a double century in a test match.
18. I decided to divide the money among Jean and June, but neither of them are anxious to have it.
19. Strolling on the beach, the sea-breeze cured my headache like it had often done.
20. The Minister for Justice has not, and probably will not introduce the Bill.
21. To descend down the steep mountain, also to carry our equipment was a task beyond us.
22. The customer complained that the article was far different and inferior to that displayed in the window.
23. I heard that the fire had broken out in the warehouse, thus causing much damage.
24. By arriving late at the theatre, there were less seats to choose from.
25. Neither he or I are in the wrong.
26. He said that when he had finished his work that he would come with me.
27. I shall not go to the station without you accompany me.
28. Who was the first to declare that the earth was round?
29. It is one of the birds that goes out for its prey at night.
30. Each set to work filling their bags with sand.

Revision Group 3

1. Each day and night were spent in preparing for the raid.
2. The reason why many crows have been shot in this district is because he is a pest.
3. The explorers were tortured by the sun's heat, which was now high in the sky.
4. The lance pierced through the knight's mail.
5. I inquired as to whether either of the dogs were for sale.
6. The soldiers will have to surrender except they receive immediate attention.
7. I said I shall go with him.
8. Can I have a lend of your racquet so that I might play in the match?
9. His parents were poor but honest.
10. Now we are getting plenty of eggs, also plenty of sugar, we will be happy.
11. "Will you help me or no?" said the tramp, who was that weak that he could not hardly stand.
12. I have received no information on the subject, neither from him nor from her.
13. Parliament has adjourned, and they will not meet again until the end of the month.
14. I have met both Barbara, Loris and Dot, but I think the latter the more charming.
15. Neither Betty or I are going to the party.
16. The explanation of his absences were because the roads were too bad for travelling.
17. This fence is no stronger, and not even as strong as the one you made last week.
18. A new member of our team was Joe Thompson, a very boastful fellow, and who became very unpopular.
19. She is one of those girls who wants her own way.
20. Neither Tom nor I have attended the last two meetings, which is most unfortunate.
21. I am sure that everybody has already and will in the future do all in their power to assist you.
22. In a fire at a nearby garage two cars were destroyed and one slightly damaged.
23. I had dinner with Shirley yesterday, and she only talked about her holiday all the evening.
24. The reason you gave was more sound than any you had previously given.
25. "Pickwick Papers" are read with pleasure by many people.
26. He is unable to fly like a bird nor swim like a fish.
27. England's happiest hour was when Winston Churchill became Prime Minister.
28. In one day he was appointed and dismissed from the position.
29. While standing near the door, a strange sight met my gaze.
30. You should not prevent him going to the picnic.

PUBLIC EXAMINATION PAPERS

(with acknowledgements)

UNIVERSITY OF LONDON: MATRICULATION

Point out the faults in the following sentences, and rewrite the passages in correct form:

1. The two men were not interested in the same things, and the chief work which each of them had to do was of a very different kind.
2. He mistrusted my youth, my commonsense, and my seamanship, and made a point of showing it in a hundred little ways.
3. I cannot help but think that the General did not fight so much by choice as by compulsion.
4. The soldiers were too exhausted to take the proper care they ought of their horses.
5. Unlike Marlborough, duty, not glory, was the mainspring of his actions.
6. I am sorry that a previous engagement will prevent me being present on Wednesday evening.
7. He will see the alterations that were proposed to be made, but rejected.
8. The nation has settled the question that it would not have conscription.
9. It was while receiving a deputation that the bullet of the anarchist struck the President.
10. Between the junction of the two tributaries was a level piece of ground on which the force encamped.

SCOTTISH EDUCATION DEPARTMENT:

LEAVING CERTIFICATE

Rewrite the following sentences in good English, explaining precisely what is wrong in each:

1. I am neither an ascetic in theory or practice.
2. A clergyman in Perthshire wishes to purchase a small pony to do the work of a minister.
3. Another bullet hit the butt of his rifle, thus saving his life.
4. Entering the drawing-room the conviction came to him that he was in the dwelling of an individual of refined taste.
5. Montmorency saw the black flag hoisted with a smile of contempt.
6. He seldom looked at the picture, which he frequently did, without shedding tears.

7. When out at sea in a vessel the horizon is always circular.

8. Erected to the memory of John Phillips accidentally shot as a mark of affection by his brother.

9. Respectful Madam,—We have pleasure in forwarding your watch by this evening's post, which is now going satisfactorily.

10. He said to his patient that, if he did not get better, he thought he had better come back to say how he was.

THE UNIVERSITY OF SCOTLAND:

PRELIMINARY EXAMINATION

Rewrite, so as to correct or improve them, the following sentences, giving reasons for any changes you may make:

1. Neither of the children reach their home after their many wanderings.

2. I never remember to have felt an event more deeply than his death.

3. We fought a most furious battle yesterday, which was in its way quite as tough, and much more serious an affair than Alma.

4. I cannot, of course, dispute with an opponent who reads what I write with so little attention.

5. Life in the town or country has its advantages and disadvantages.

6. Neither my habits nor constitution are improved by your customs or climate.

7. It had been my intention to have called on you when in town, but the astonishing variety of sights have usurped my time.

8. He ate the black and white puddings, and declared he was one of those who never hesitate to gratify his desires, when opportunity offers.

9. Leonard de Courcy, a young man of a worthless character and who had just obtained a commission in the army, seemed to be very popular with every member of the family.

10. I am told that when he died the Cardinal at least spoke ten languages.

VICTORIAN EDUCATION DEPARTMENT:

INTERMEDIATE EXAMINATION

Correct the following sentences and explain why they are wrong:

1. Having given his listeners an outline of the story they may want to hear the end of it.

2. She is the elder of the four sisters, but if any one mentions the fact she is very angry with them.

3. This question is easier than last year.

4. He much preferred playing than to watch.

5. The announcer was late in giving the forecast of the weather that evening, and the latter caused great inconvenience though the former was not to blame.

6. He wrote a book which, if it had not been written, we would not have known of his experiences in Java.

7. Hastily summoning an ambulance, the corpse was driven to the mortuary.

8. We can offer you a dining-table which will seat twelve persons with round legs, or, if you prefer, fourteen persons with square legs.

9. They followed the climbers step by step through the telescopes.

10. The conspirators then dispersed with the arranged time of meeting the following morning.

11. After looking for some time at the distant object it appeared to me to be a child.

12. On one side you saw the steep cliff, and shuddered at the thought of the dreadful end one would have if they fell over the edge.

13. He arose early and left the house where he had stayed for the night on his bicycle.

14. Although yellow with age we could read the faint hand writing on the document.

15. The man was suspiciously carrying a black bag.

16. He writes in such a temper that he seems first to grind the sentences between his teeth, which he then puts down on paper.

17. My wages were withheld, not having done the prescribed duty.

VICTORIAN EDUCATION DEPARTMENT:

INTERMEDIATE EXAMINATION

Correct or improve the following sentences:

1. He is one of those boys who is always late.
2. She is the girl whom I believe was chosen to represent the school.
3. We soon hope to have a new swimming pool.
4. Of the two evils, I prefer the least.
5. Knowing all the circumstances, it was necessary for Jim to deal with the problem.
6. No one likes to be left by themselves in the dark.
7. The man whom I thought was reading was really fast asleep.
8. Neither of them were able to lift the weight.
9. He took the ball off the captain and gave it to his opponent.
10. She hit it that hard that it went over the fence.
11. Sitting on the top of the Pyramids, the camels looked very tired.
12. John was a most unique child.
13. It was me who told him about his uncles accident and because of his distress I remained with him for a few hours. Hoping to take his mind off his worries, it was suggested that he make a cup of tea. Later on there were less tears.
14. Let him and I settle who to invite.
15. Do you mind me having the loan of your book?
16. The speed of the wind is very great and travels at about one hundred miles an hour.
17. Seeing the rocket, the lifeboat put out, manned by its heroic crew.
18. I have three sisters neither of which is any good at tennis.
19. If the pictures in your drawing-room are not liked by your family, hang them upstairs.
20. He is taller than me.
21. Between you and I, there's not much chance of them passing this year.
22. It will be easy to get in as the new doorkeeper don't care who he admits.
23. Hardly had the bell sounded than the children trooped out of school.
24. The climate of England is not as good as Australia.
25 Every sane person ought to make their country better than any in the world.

NEW SOUTH WALES EDUCATION DEPARTMENT:

LEAVING CERTIFICATE EXAMINATION

Make any alterations you think desirable in the following sentences, and explain as carefully as you can why you are making them:

1. I am one of those who cannot describe what I feel.
2. Turning the corner at full speed, a slight bump in the road lifted the car and disaster ensued.
3. Internationalism is good in theory, but it is natural for everyone to prefer their own country.
4. The name of Rupert Brooke will never be without honour, but if he had survived the war he may have become one of our greatest poets.
5. The second assault was met by Buckingham by a counter attack on the Earl of Bristol whom, he knew, would be the chief witness against him.
6. He is reading a letter to his father.
7. Some people will worry about nothing.
8. The exercises are intended to develop flabby muscles.
9. The charge of stealing at the request of the lad's employer was dropped.
10. The speaker strongly objected to the unfounded suggestion that speed and speed alone was the sole cause which accounted for the recent increase in the number of motor accidents which had lately occurred on the roads.
11. The unit produces cold air by collecting air from the hot engine; compresses it, and then letting it expand so that it cools below freezing point.
12. Many people who had so far travelled happily along the highroads of buoyancy were all too ready to assume that business, industry and full employment were at last foundering in the ditch.
13. Sin is what you know is right and don't do.
14. Some means will have to be found to arrest the upward tendency of retail price levels.
15. The government departments here are honeycombed with crooks and gorged with grafters.
16. Television influences opinion through day-to-day facial editorialisation, potent in terms of the amount of hero-worship, the viewer feels for the personality on the screen.
17. Butter may be quite satisfactorily substituted by margarine.

NEW SOUTH WALES EDUCATION DEPARTMENT: LEAVING CERTIFICATE EXAMINATION

Rewrite the following sentences, making any changes that you consider necessary. Explain clearly why you are making them.

1. An endless stream of cars have been passing for the last two hours.

2. If he has committed this offence, he deserved to be punished.

3. Tell me whom you think is likely to win this match.

4. Nobody reading a satire will ever apply the author's criticisms to themselves personally.

5. We gathered firewood and piled it near the door, so that the fire could be replenished without leaving the hut.

6. I think he would make a better golfer than other sports.

7. The association would and has taken action to discover whom should be held responsible.

8. If I go to the pictures, I would probably have been bored.

9. Cynthia said she was afraid she cannot come to the party because she will be on holidays then.

10. Anyone who has not bought their tickets have no chance of being admitted.

11. The members of the committee which has been set up to examine parking plans for the city has not been able to reach a decision.

12. Whom do you think will take over as captain of the First Eleven.

13. If he does not succeed it will not be because the task is too hard, but will be due to his own laziness.

14. Too sudden a change of temperature in the case of most people are likely to cause chills.

15. The end result of the drought is not likely to be productive of much serious loss.

NEW SOUTH WALES DEPARTMENT OF
TECHNICAL EDUCATION:
CERTIFICATE ENTRANCE

Say what you think is wrong with the following sentences, and rewrite them as you think they should be written:

1. Neither the boy nor his brother have been seen since morning.
2. He is one of those persons who is always chattering.
3. He is not as tall as me.
4. Everyone should do their best.
5. I do not like these kind of questions.
6. The property was shared equally between the five children.
7. Between you and I he was wrong in what he said.
8. He should of seen a doctor.
9. A mob of unruly bullocks were yarded for the rodeo.
10. The officer as well as the men were mentioned in dispatches.
11. We laid down in the long grass.
12. Neither of the two machines are wanted.
13. A new set of engine parts were delivered this morning.
14. He was hit by a stone riding a bike.
15. Jim does not know the girl who I met yesterday.
16. The reason why I do this is because I want to, that's all.
17. The murderer was hung at 8 o'clock.

NEW SOUTH WALES DEPARTMENT OF TECHNICAL EDUCATION: QUALIFYING AND MATRICULATION COURSES

Say what you think is wrong with the following sentences, and rewrite them as you think they should be written:

1. The accountant paid £50 to the widow of the man who was drowned by order of the committee.

2. A box of apples were stolen by the boys this morning.

3. I only wrote four letters this morning.

4. Mr. Jones saw a kangaroo looking out of the carriage window.

5. Having gone out for a walk the sun came out and made it enjoyable.

6. If I were him I should act different.

7. On him revealing his fear of Caesar's aspirations Cassius proceeds to draw him into the conspiracy.

8. The essayist had forgotten the fact that we are made up of individuality when he wrote this essay even in childhood.

9. Many articles which upon looking back, must seem trivial were real precious.

10. The minister when faced with the problem of reducing taxation, he refused to commit himself in any fixed policy.

11. Following the president's opening remarks, the building was thrown open for inspection.

12. Another subject that the Home Secretary will be asked to consider, and doubtless will be introduced in the same Bill, will be that of monopolies.

13. According to reliable sources, one-third of the population are living in sub-standard houses, which is very possibly true.

14. He worked hard with a view to going to the University by means of a scholarship, but found that in order to do so he would have to improve his prose style.

15. Educated at an American university General Sun was himself wounded in eleven places in fighting at Shanghai in 1937.

16. While engaged in buying a new hat the man's bicycle was stolen.

17. Lady Macbeth, she is far more superior than her husband, but her affectionate love towards him was very deep.

CAMBRIDGE GENERAL CERTIFICATE OF EDUCATION
(ORDINARY LEVEL)

Each of the following sentences contains one error. Rewrite the sentence correctly.

1. Being hot, the ice-cream pleased me greatly.
2. The reason why we were late was because the car broke down.
3. Although the lecture was on his favourite subject, he appeared to be completely disinterested in it.
4. He deposited his suit-case down on the platform.
5. There is a space between every house in this street.
6. Fold it carefully, like he told us.
7. I should have liked to have seen that match.
8. All the boys were good cricketers, but none of them were suitable for the captaincy of the team.

Each of the following sentences contains two errors of grammar, structure or vocabulary. Rewrite the sentences correctly. Make no alterations except those necessitated by your corrections, and do not change the intended meaning of the sentences.

1. Due to faulty planning, thousands of pounds were literally poured down the drain.
2. I am one of those sort of people who cannot praise what I dislike.
3. The climate of Australia is as good or even better than England.
4. Most of the witnesses, including my brother and I, collaborated the defendant's evidence.
5. He was a better athlete than any boy in his class and not only hoped to win the race but also to break the record.
6. The name of the girl whom he understood was to partake in the final was Elsie.
7. The committee is comprised of seven members and they each have one vote.
8. If you'd have been there, you would have agreed that there were considerably less spectators than usual.
9. He thought it was rather a unique little town, and he grew so fond of it that after his death he said he would like to be buried there.
10. John and Arthur's attitude towards compulsory games are exactly the same.

OXFORD AND CAMBRIDGE SCHOOLS EXAMINATION BOARD: GENERAL CERTIFICATE OF EDUCATION (ORDINARY LEVEL)

Correct any mistakes you find in the following sentences:

1. I like these sort of chocolates more than the others, but either kind are welcome.
2. He immediately picked out the boy whom he thought had stolen the childrens sweets.
3. Due to the bad weather, the two last weeks of the holidays were very dull.
4. When looking round the house, the new furniture impressed my sister and I very much.
5. As a result of the fine weather, I shouldn't be surprised, if our well didn't dry up.
6. I should be delighted, if you will come to dinner with me.
7. Crossing the bridge, a fine prospect unfolded itself.
8. By saying that he was too fond of games, the Housemaster inferred that Brown did not work hard enough.
9. The engagement will be announced next week, but that information is strictly between you and I.
10. He drove passed in an old car wearing a top hat and a blue overcoat.
11. Throughout his long professional career he always has and still does take a nap every afternoon.
12. Having cut off his leg, the doctor promised to instruct the patient as to how to use an artificial one.
13. Neither the captain or the vice-captain were in their best form to-day.
14. If either of these schemes miscarry, it will be necessary for you or I to step into the breach.
15. Being an only son, his death is doubly tragic.
16. Hardly had he left than the roof fell in.
17. The man who I met yesterday had a new motor car but which unfortunately broke down this morning.
18. The tale he told me was so incredible that it was neither believed by me or my brother.
19. The river has overflown its banks.
20. Whom do you think is to blame?
21. The liner could be seen leaving port from the cliffs, all it's flags flying.
22. The test is not meant for people like you and I.

GREAT BRITAIN AND IRELAND:
CIVIL SERVICE: NAVY, ARMY AND AIR-FORCE
ENTRANCE EXAMINATIONS

The following sentences contain errors of grammar, usage, vocabulary, punctuation and expression. Say what you think are the faults in each of these sentences, and write out a corrected version in clear, precise English:

1. He compared his brother to the boy next door to see who was the tallest.
2. The men's clothes were not only soaked by the rain but they also contracted severe colds.
3. Anyone can be expected to strongly object to being asked to agree to accept a salary inferior to what they are used to.
4. I and my friends were often in the habit of going to the cinema on Saturday afternoon.
5. In this great danger everyone seemed to try and find out who he could help and thought of others rather than of themselves.
6. The question is to send the report without him seeing it.
7. The reason the car arrived late was, because it's driver could not either remember the name of the street or the number of the house.
8. One of the council by-laws state that the space between each house must be sufficient for the eventful erection of a garage.
9. The roses made a finer if not the finest display than I had seen before.
10. The sub-committee is comprised of five ordinary members an honourable treasurer and a chairman which meets on the two first days of each month.
11. When sleeping soundly, a loud alarm clock can give one a most unpleasant reminder that it is time you got up.
12. Between you and i said john he meant to infer that these sort of arguments seem to only aggravate our neighbours.
13. Our mutual liking for jazz will, like I said, cement our friendship into full bloom.
14. It soon became only too clear that the witness was not only not telling all that he could have done about the incident but was also obviously adopting a hostile attitude to the Court as well.
15. Neither the motorist or the pedestrian were to blame for the tragic accident whose occurrence was owing to icy road conditions.

GREAT BRITAIN AND IRELAND:
CIVIL SERVICE EXAMINATIONS:
CLERICAL DIVISION

The following sentences could be expressed more accurately and clearly, by avoiding jargon, for example, or errors of grammar, vocabulary, spelling and punctuation. Say what you think are the faults in each of these sentences, and write out a corrected version of each in clear, precise English.

1. Knowing little about music the military band failed to interest me even though comprised of a hundred players.
2. My accomadation is terrible because the rooms have not been properly cleaned for ages.
3. This year I thought the roses in my friends garden as good if not better than last year.
4. Can you direct me to the girls grammar school please I would rather prefer to walk but I will take a bus if the rout runs passed the school.
5. That type of people are very obstinate the keeper said when the trespassers refused to believe that they could be persecuted.
6. He was given a stimulus of brandy but his pulse was no different after than before.
7. Due to him coming into the business world when he was older than me he has not got either the training or the experience as I have.
8. Looking at the problem from all angles, it is difficult to prophecy what the eventual outcome shall be.
9. Few have understood it like you have done and the reason why is because the study of these new subjects demand a keen intelligence.
10. In one of the best books that has ever been written, there were pilgrims going to Canterbury in company on horseback due to robbers on the way.
11. The lawyer was agreed that the rumour was libellous, and could not be repeated.
12. Which would you rather that the lion should eat you or the tiger.
13. The luxurious growth of the tropical forest said he is a sight to be seen.
14. What legal sanction has the well-known warning sign keep off the grass in public parks.
15. When asked if he would support the motion, it was clear that he was embarassed, also that he was unwilling to say no.
16. Due to a sceptic finger he was unable to even draw a paralell line.

SHADES OF MEANING

Explain carefully the shades of meaning of the following bracketed words. Use the words in sentences to illustrate the meanings:

e.g., (a) ask, beg, demand.

These three words denote a type of asking. "Ask" is used when that which is wanted is easily granted; "beg" when the something desired is obtained with difficulty; and "demand" when there is determination to have.

(i) Frequently strangers *ask* the way to the station.

(ii) "I *beg* this favour of you," pleaded the condemned man.

(iii) "We *demand* our rights," shouted the angry citizens.

(b) accompany, attend, escort.

The action of accompanying is contained in these three words. We "accompany" our equals with whom we wish to go; we "attend" our superiors whom we desire to serve; and we "escort" those whom we are obliged to protect.

(i) We may *accompany* our friends on their next trip.

(ii) These are the persons who will *attend* the Queen during her tour.

(iii) A strong bodyguard will *escort* the distinguished foreign visitor.

GROUP 1

{ gobble	{ bruise	{ battle
munch	scar	war
{ peck	{ wound	{ duel
{ warm	{ cool	{ friend
hot	cold	acquaintance
{ boiling	{ chilly	{ ally

GROUP 2

{ laugh
  grin
  giggle

{ branch
  twig
  trunk

{ town
  city
  capital

{ cry
  weep
  sob

{ cottage
  cabin
  mansion

{ bad
  wicked
  naughty

GROUP 3

{ bush
  forest
  jungle

{ mud
  silt
  slush

{ angry
  annoyed
  furious

{ drink
  sip
  swallow

{ dirty
  soiled
  filthy

{ scrub
  wipe
  polish

GROUP 4

Can you name the creatures that make the following distinctive noises?

roar	buzz	squeak
bellow	neigh	mew
bark	purr	hoot
bray	bleat	caw
quack	gobble	whinny
grunt	chirp	bay
snort	croak	twitter

GROUP 5

{ perfume
  smell
  stench

{ shrunken
  squat
  stunted

{ bob
  bounce
  skip

{ brim
  brink
  brow

{ clip
  reap
  prune

{ watch
  sun-dial
  clock

GROUP 6

{ tease irritate ill-treat	{ street track highway	{ rap thump slog
{ few rare scarce	{ fade perish wither	{ big large immense

GROUP 7

{ meal feast luncheon	{ brave daring reckless	{ grasp clasp snatch
{ shake tremble shudder	{ weak feeble helpless	{ bake grill stew

GROUP 8

Tell what you know of the following "habitation words":

hutch	bungalow	palace
stable	teepee	wigwam
lair	hut	igloo
stall	homestead	cell
kennel	hovel	pen
sty	castle	coop
shanty	flat	eyrie

GROUP 9

{ colour shade tinge	{ bridge gangway viaduct	{ wind breeze gust
{ moist soggy swampy	{ pupil student disciple	{ drowsy weary exhausted

GROUP 10

{ muffle quieten stifle	{ fumble grope paw	{ firm fixed solid
{ dip plunge wallow	{ list slope tilt	{ greet hail salute

GROUP 11

Give a description of the following "receptacle words," and state their uses:

crate	granary	bassinet
hod	canister	holster
keg	armoury	quiver
scabbard	tumbler	knapsack
vat	bin	till
magazine	trunk	locker
wallet	casket	chest

GROUP 12

{ goal limit outcome	{ write scribble copy	{ dishearten hamper prevent
{ directly immediately instantly	{ cheating treachery treason	{ consider inspect overhaul

GROUP 13

{ aid incite uphold	{ loose lax slack	{ transfer unload vacate
{ awkward gawky bungling	{ reduce relieve remove	{ circular poster advertisement

GROUP 14

bribe donation grant	satisfaction glee fun	disturb disorganize disarrange
ache twinge agony	gather hoard pile	strong powerful invincible

GROUP 15

recite address debate	brand singe cremate	dray stage-coach chariot
church cathedral chapel	gush squirt trickle	song lullaby hymn

GROUP 16

Write sentences appropriately using the following "sound words":

chime	trill	boom
clatter	whine	wheeze
hum	crackle	gurgle
patter	crash	clang
peal	clash	rustle
rattle	jingle	crunch
rumble	click	drum

GROUP 17

river tributary stream	stain spot smudge	apology excuse confession
stare glare glance	race nation tribe	invade charge besiege

GROUP 18

{ burglar highwayman bushranger	{ meadow prairie scrub	{ replace displace substitute
{ master overpower overthrow	{ tenant boarder guest	{ murder manslaughter suicide

GROUP 19

{ defeat conquer rout	{ throw toss heave	{ please delight interest
{ arcade cloister aisle	{ fleet squadron armada	{ ash ashes embers

GROUP 20

The following words express slow movement. Write sentences illustrating their uses.

stroll	saunter	waddle
crawl	shuffle	strut
creep	slouch	sidle
dawdle	stagger	sneak
hobble	toddle	slink
limp	totter	stalk
plod	trudge	lumber

GROUP 21

Here is a list of words expressing rapid movement. Write sentences illustrating their uses.

dart	skim	hurtle
flit	sweep	dash
gallop	prance	scurry
scamper	streak	plunge
scud	slither	scramble
scuttle	swoop	hustle

GROUP 22

wave ripple roller	bail ladle spoon	shore coast beach
pull drag tow	lift raise hoist	repair rebuild remodel

GROUP 23

escape evade elude	dumb silent tongue-tied	hop leap spring
hideous ungainly misshapen	chew gnaw nibble	high tall lofty

GROUP 24

body corpse carcass	stun startle electrify	shapely ornamental handsome
sensible wise shrewd	book volume pamphlet	turn twist warp

GROUP 25

character reputation record	kind humane indulgent	confer consult discuss
inherit acquire earn	strive undertake attempt	rotate circle swirl

GROUP 26

When would you use the following as verbs of "saying"?

splutter	squeal	whine
mumble	snap	snivel
blubber	gasp	snarl
scream	warn	mutter
whisper	pipe	wail
object	plead	moan
groan	sigh	whimper

GROUP 27

{ punish retaliate revenge	{ amity unison unity	{ glut surplus profusion
{ effeminate womanish womanly	{ masculine mannish manly	{ freedom independence licence

GROUP 28

{ old ancient antique obsolete	{ painter sketcher cartoonist draughtsman	{ whittle hew hack slice
{ abandon desert resign abdicate	{ thief swindler counterfeiter shop-lifter	{ peer distinguish survey scan

GROUP 29

{ voyage tour pilgrimage ramble	{ inform teach advise dictate	{ allowance payment salary wages

{ electrocute
hang
guillotine
behead

{ majestic
dignified
stately
pompous

{ neglect
forget
ignore
overlook

GROUP 30

{ opponent
enemy
assailant
rival

{ shelter
refuge
asylum
sanctuary

{ dig
grub
exhume
excavate

{ strict
unreasonable
cruel
relentless

{ choice
alternative
preference
selection

{ publication
announcement
broadcast
message

GROUP 31

{ oscillate
revolve
rock
jolt

{ tragedy
misfortune
disaster
casualty

{ weather
climate
temperature
atmosphere

{ work
toil
drudgery
slavery

{ bonus
legacy
honorarium
subsidy

{ tolerate
respect
appreciate
revere

GROUP 32

{ pleasure
rejoicing
happiness
ecstasy

{ attractive
fascinating
enchanting
beautiful

{ abscond
bolt
elope
retreat

{ sell
barter
trade
bargain

{ silly
stupid
ridiculous
absurd

{ entertainment
relaxation
hobby
sport

GROUP 33

desire longing liking craving	graceful poised elegant becoming	vice sin crime · fault
alter change amend improve	loyalty faithfulness homage obedience	great famous well-known celebrated

GROUP 34

award endow compensate bequeath	occupation profession trade job	sleep nap siesta hibernation
impure tainted offensive musty	split crack shatter smash	period reign decade generation

GROUP 35

uncommon unnatural extraordinary unique	dim dark obscure murky	mutiny rebellion riot strike
love affection fondness devotion	release acquit ransom unfetter	mean paltry vile despicable

GROUP 36

compliment praise flattery applause	small minute tiny microscopic	pity sympathy mercy tenderness

- noise
- tumult
- din
- uproar

- blame
- censure
- condemn
- sentence

- costly
- valuable
- precious
- priceless

GROUP 37

- ill-bred
- coarse
- insulting
- blunt

- insane
- crazy
- delirious
- rambling

- exile
- deport
- expel
- discharge

- politician
- statesman
- minister
- dictator

- clever
- gifted
- expert
- dextrous

- conversation
- dialogue
- chat
- gossip

GROUP 38

- sullen
- morose
- surly
- moody

- carnival
- revelry
- orgy
- festival

- young
- youthful
- puerile
- adolescent

- sack
- pillage
- steal
- rifle

- astonishment
- awe
- bewilderment
- admiration

- think
- reflect
- ponder
- muse

GROUP 39

- rapacious
- greedy
- covetous
- niggardly

- blunder
- error
- omission
- oversight

- wondrous
- inexplicable
- unexpected
- phenomenal

- curious
- inquiring
- inquisitive
- prying

- jubilee
- celebration
- solemnization
- commemoration

- disappointment
- chagrin
- discontent
- dissatisfaction

GROUP 40

- courtly
- cultured
- polite
- civil

- ailment
- indisposition
- disease
- infirmity

- contract
- treaty
- stipulation
- transaction

{ criticize
  chide
  abuse
  reprimand

{ healthy
  healthful
  wholesome
  salubrious

{ hospitable
  philanthropic
  generous
  humanitarian

GROUP 41

{ undignified
  contemptible
  disrespectful
  infamous

{ slander
  libel
  vilify
  reproach

{ harmful
  pernicious
  detrimental
  destructive

{ bemoan
  mourn
  bewail
  lament

{ adventurous
  bold
  valiant
  heroic

{ nervous
  cowed
  frightened
  terrified

GROUP 42

{ deride
  mock
  scorn
  chaff

{ anecdotes
  annals
  chronicles
  memoirs

{ dispute
  controversy
  wrangle
  squabble

{ hatred
  aversion
  dislike
  loathing

{ vague
  ambiguous
  puzzling
  fallacious

{ capricious
  vacillating
  irresolute
  restless

GROUP 43

{ emaciated
  wizened
  debilitated
  decrepit

{ haughty
  supercilious
  arrogant
  vain

{ disobedient
  insubordinate
  undutiful
  contumacious

{ regret
  sorrow
  remorse
  repentance

{ irony
  sarcasm
  satire
  wit

{ restore
  revive
  renovate
  rejuvenate

Other Educational Publications
by
W. FOSTER, M.A.
and
H. BRYANT, B.A.

Obtainable from all Educational Booksellers in Australasia
Sole Wholesale Distributors:
ANTHONY HORDERN & SONS LTD., Sydney

COMPREHENSION AND COMPOSITION, BOOK I
New and enlarged edition for secondary classes. Treats all aspects of comprehension and composition work. 160 pages.

COMPREHENSION AND COMPOSITION, BOOK II
New and enlarged edition for secondary classes. Further work in all aspects of comprehension and composition work. 160 pages.

COMPREHENSION AND COMPOSITION, BOOK III
All aspects of comprehension and composition work for students (14-16 years). 160 pages.

SELECTED POEMS FOR AUSTRALIAN SCHOOLS
New and enlarged edition with explanatory notes. An anthology of English, American and Australian poems. For First and Second Year classes. 144 pages.

A BOOK OF VERSE FOR AUSTRALIAN SCHOOLS
A sequel to "Selected Poems for Australian Schools." Contents include twenty-three English and thirty-two Australian poems, with biographies and notes. 128 pages.

THE GATEWAY TO SHAKESPEARE
Abridged Shakespearean plays, with textual, acting and costuming notes. Thirty-seven illustrations. 160 pages.

SOHRAB AND RUSTUM, *by* Matthew Arnold
Complete text, edited with introduction, notes and questions.

THE RIME OF THE ANCIENT MARINER, *by* S. T. Coleridge
Complete text, edited with introduction, notes and questions.

ATALANTA'S RACE, *by* William Morris
Complete text, edited with introduction, notes and questions.

THE MAN BORN TO BE KING, *by* William Morris
Complete text, edited with introduction, notes and questions.

A PRECIS BOOK FOR AUSTRALIAN SCHOOLS
Fifty-four literary excerpts, chosen for their aptness as precis passages, and for comprehension and appreciation exercises.